SPEISEKARTE

Insight Phrase Book

German

Original text: Elisabeth Graf-Riemann
Editor: Sabine von Loeffelholz
English edition translated by: Paul Fletcher
Edited by: Renée Holler and Hannah Rees

Managing Editor: Tony Halliday
Editorial Director: Brian Bell

CONTACTING THE EDITORS: As every effort is made to provide accurate information in this publication, we would appreciate it if readers would call our attention to any errors and omissions by contacting:
Apa Publications, PO Box 7910, London SE1 1WE, England.
Fax: (44 20) 7403 0290
e-mail: insight@apaguide.demon.co.uk

1st edition 2000

Printed in Singapore by Insight Print Services (Pte) Ltd

Distributed in the UK & Ireland by:
GeoCenter International Ltd
The Viables Centre, Harrow Way, Basingstoke,
Hampshire RG22 4BJ
Tel: (44 1256) 817987, Fax: (44 1256) 817-988

Distributed in the United States by:
Langenscheidt Publishers, Inc.
46–35 54th Road, Maspeth, NY 11378
Tel: (1 718) 784-0055, Fax: (1 718) 784-0640

Worldwide distribution enquiries:
APA Publications GmbH & Co. Verlag KG (Singapore Branch)
38 Joo Koon Road, Singapore 628990
Tel: (65) 865-1600, Fax: (65) 861-6438

INSIGHT PHRASE BOOK

German

Apa Publications

Contents

Introduction

About this book

Insight Phrase Books are the perfect companion when touring abroad as they cover all the everyday situations faced by travellers who are not familiar with the language of their holiday hosts.

The sentences and expressions translated here have been chosen carefully so that you can make yourself understood quickly and easily. You will not find any complicated sentence constructions or long word lists. Nearly all the sentences have been compiled from basic phrases so that by substituting words and other expressions, you will be able to cope with a variety of conversational situations.

The word lists at the end of each section are themed and this will make it easy for you to vary what you want to say. You will be able to make yourself understood quickly in the foreign language with the minimum vocabulary. You won't need to spend a long time searching for the word you want.

So that you can understand what others are saying to you in everyday situations, e.g. at the doctor, at the border, we have marked with a * those phrases and questions that you are likely to hear frequently.

A simplified pronunciation guide geared towards English speakers will help you to say correctly the words you need. You will also find a summary of basic pronunciation information, together with a brief introduction to German grammar.

This introduction is followed by nine chapters containing examples of sentences from general and tourist-related situations. You will find general tips and guidance not just in the chapter entitled Practical Information, but elsewhere in the book too. The various feature boxes contain useful information on such matters as meal times, using public transport and telephones, the different categories of hotels and restaurants and lots more.

At the end of the book you will find an English-German dictionary, which can be used for reference and as an index, the page number referring to an entry in one of the nine chapters. The German-English dictionary contains a selection of important words and abbreviations, which you are likely to encounter on signs, notices and information boards.

Hoping you have lots of fun on your travels and Gute Reise! [**goo**tuh **riy**zuh] *(Have a good trip!)*.

Pronunciation

All the German words included in this guide are given a phonetic rendering. This always appears in square brackets after the translation and there is only one special symbol to remember. You will see that where a word has more than one syllable, the stressed syllable is shown in bold, e.g. Hafen [**hah**fen] *(harbour)*, Samstag [**zams**tahg] *(Saturday)*.

Although the phonetic rendering can be read as though it were English, the following points about pronunciation should be noted:

Vowels

- short **a** as in bad, e.g. Mann [man] *(husband)*
- long **a** as in father, Abend [**ah**bent] *(evening)*
- short **e** as in bed, e.g. nett [net] *(nice)*
- long **e** as in they, e.g. Esel [ayzel] *(donkey)*

- short **i** as bit, e.g. Schiff [shif] *(ship)*
- long **i** as in seek, e.g. Liter [**lee**ter] *(litre)*
- short **o** as in not, e.g. Koch [kokh] (chef)
- long **o** as in nose, e.g. wo [voh] *(where)*
- short **u** as in could, e.g. dunkel [doonkel] *(dark)*
- long **u** as in boot, e.g. Juni [**yoo**nee] *(June)*

Umlauts

The double dot above three of the five vowels is known as an umlaut. It has the effect of adding an **e** to the vowel.

- **ä** as in get, e.g. Gepäck [ge**pek**] *(luggage)*
- **ö** as in her, e.g. schön [shern] *(beautiful)*
- **ü** has no English parallel. It is like the French tu. Say the English word few but with the lips rounded and pushed forward. Example: über [**ew**ber] *(above)*
- **y** makes the same sound as **ü** e.g. zynisch [**tsew**nish] *(cynical)*

Then there are the dipthong sounds:

- **ai** as in tie, e.g. Saite [**ziy**tuh] *(string)*
- **au** as in how, e.g. sauer [**zow**er] *(sour)*
- **ie** as in thief, e.g. Dieb [deep] *(thief)*
- **ei** as in wine, e.g. Wein [viyn] *(wine)*
- **eu/äu** as in boil, e.g. Feuer [**foy**uh] *(fire)*

Consonants

Most consonants are pronounced as in English but with the following exceptions:

- **b** is pronounced as a **p** when it is the final letter of the word, e.g. Stab [stahp] *(pole)*
- **d** is pronounced as a **t** when it is the final letter in a word, e.g. gesund [ge**zoont**] *(healthy)*
- **g** always as in get
- **ch** as in the German composer Bach or the Scottish loch. Example: Mädchen [**mayd**khen] *(girl)*
- **j** is pronounced like a **y**, e.g. Jäger [**yay**ger] *(hunter)*
- **k** is pronounced even before an n, e.g. Kneipe [**kniy**puh] *(pub)*
- **v** is more like an English **f**, e.g. Vater [**fah**ter] *(father)*
- **w** is like the English **v**, e.g. Wagen [**vah**gen] *(car)*
- **z** is pronounced as **ts**, e.g. Zimmer [**tsi**mmer] *(room)*

The s

Before a vowel s is pronounced like the z in zoo, e.g. singen [**zi**ngen] *(to sing)*
Before the consonants p or t, the s becomes sh, e.g. Stück [shtewk] *(piece)*
At the end of a word the s is soft and pronounced as in sale, e.g. Hals [hals] *(neck)*
The "scharfes S" symbol ß equates to ss and is always soft, e.g. Straße [**shtrah**suh] *(street)*.

Stress

The rules about stress for words of two or more syllables are complicated. Usually it is the first syllable which is stressed, but there are many exceptions. In this book the stressed syllable is shown in bold type. Example: Freundschaft [**froy**ndshaft] *(friendship)*.

The German alphabet

A a	[ah]	N n	[enn]
B b	[bay]	O o	[oh]
C c	[tsay]	P p	[pay]
D d	[day]	Q q	[koo]
E e	[eh]	R r	[air]
F f	[eff]	S s	[ess]
G g	[gay]	T t	[tay]
H h	[har]	U u	[oo]
I i	[ee]	V v	[fow]
J j	[yot]	W w	[vay]
K k	[kar]	X x	[icks]
L l	[ell]	Y y	[**ewp**silon]
M m	[emm]	Z z	[tset]

Grammar

The German language presents certain difficulties. For example, nouns have three genders and four cases, the word order in sentences is governed by some complicated rules and there are five different ways to say "the". However, pronunciation is generally perfectly consistent with spelling.

The article

Nouns can be either masculine, feminine or neuter gender.

Gender and the definite article

masculine singular:
der Mann [dair man] *(the man)*
masculine plural:
die Männer [dee **men**ner] *(the men)*

feminine singular:
die Frau [dee frow] *(the woman)*
feminine plural:
die Frauen [dee **frow**en] *(the women)*

neuter singular:
das Lied [das leet] *(the song)*
neuter plural:
die Lieder [dee **lee**der] *(the songs)*

Gender and the indefinite article

masculine singular:
ein Mann [iyn man] *(a man)*
masculine plural:
einige Männer [**iy**niguh **men**ner] *(some men)*

feminine singular:
eine Frau [**iy**nuh frow] *(a woman)*
feminine plural:
einige Frauen [**iy**niguh **frow**en] *(some women)*

neuter singular:
ein Lied [iyn leet] *(a song)*

neuter plural:
einige Lieder [**iy**niguh **lee**der] *(some songs)*

Case

The definite and indefinite article change their form to agree with the noun. Shown above are the articles' nominative forms, i.e. the subject or initiator of an action or speech. The accusative form reflects the person or thing directly affected by the action, genitive indicates possession and the dative form shows the recipient of the action.

Declination of the definite article

masculine:
Nom. der [dair] *(the)*
Acc. den [dayn] *(the)*
Gen. des [des] *(of the)*
Dat. dem [daym] *(to the)*

feminine:
Nom. die [dee] *(the)*
Acc. die [dee] *(the)*
Gen. der [dair] *(of the)*
Dat. der [dair] *(to the)*

neuter:
Nom. das [das] *(the)*
Acc. das [das] *(the)*
Gen. des [dair] *(of the)*
Dat. dem [daym] *(to the)*

plural for all genders:
Nom. die [dee] *(the)*
Acc. die [dee] *(the)*
Gen. der [dair] *(of the)*
Dat. den [dayn] *(to the)*

Declination of the indefinite article

masculine:
Nom. ein [iyn] *(a)*
Acc. einen [**iy**nen] *(a)*
Gen. eines [**iy**nes] *(of a)*
Dat. einem [**iy**nem] *(to a)*

feminine:
Nom. eine [**iy**nuh] *(a)*
Acc. eine [**iy**nuh] *(a)*
Gen. einer [**iy**ner] *(of a)*
Dat. einer [**iy**ner] *(to a)*

neuter:
Nom. ein [iyn] *(a)*
Acc. ein [iyn] *(a)*
Gen. eines [**iy**nes] *(of a)*
Dat. einem [**iy**nem] *(to a)*

Nouns

All nouns in German begin with a capital letter. Most nouns ending in -en and -er are masculine, e.g. der Garten [dair **gar**ten] *(the garden)*, der Mechaniker [dair me**kha**niker] *(mechanic)*. All nouns with endings in -schaft, -heit, -keit, -ung are feminine, as are many ending in -e. Nouns ending with -in indicate the feminine form, e.g. die Freundin (from der Freund) [dee **froyn**din] *(girlfriend)*. All nouns ending in -chen and -lein are neuter, regardless of the meaning of the word, e.g. das Fräulein [das **froy**liyn] *(the young lady)*. Nouns are also declined. However, the rules on how to decline German nouns are quite complicated and have been omitted.

Forming plurals

In German only a few nouns form their plural with -s or -es. To form the nominative plural from the nominative singular, the ending -e, -er -or -en may be added or it may be left unchanged. In some cases the root vowel may be changed to an umlaut, e.g. das Dorf [das dorf] *(the village)* becomes die Dörfer [dee **der**fer] *(the villages)*.

Adjectives

The adjective always precedes the noun. Its ending depends on whether it follows the definite or indefinite article or has no article at all, e.g. der alte Mann [dair **al**tuh man] *(the old man)* or ein alter Mann [iyn **al**tair man] *(an old man)*.

Comparison of adjectives

Apart from a few exceptions, adjectives form their comparatives and superlatives by adding -(e)r and -(e)st, e.g. klein [kliyn] *(small)*, kleiner [**kliy**ner] *(smaller)*, kleinste [**kliy**nstuh] *(smallest)*. Many single-syllable adjectives with the stem vowel a, o or u have an umlaut ä, ö and ü in the comparative and superlative, e.g. alt [alt] *(old)*, älter [**el**ter] *(older)*, älteste [**el**testuh] *(oldest)*.

For direct comparisons use "als", e.g. Sie ist hübscher als ihre Schwester [zee ist **hewb**sher als **ih**ruh **shve**ster] *(she is prettier than her sister)*.

Adverbs

Some adverbs are formed by adding a suffix to the adjective, often -lich or -weise, e.g. sicherlich [**zik**herlikh] *(safely)*; glücklicherweise [glewklikher**viy**zuh] *(fortunately)*. However, most adjectives can be used without change, eg Sie singt gut [zee zingt goot] *(she sings well)*.

Pronouns

There are three ways of addressing people in German with the word "you". One is the polite, formal way (Sie), the other more informal (du). Ihr is the plural form of du. Du and ihr are used between friends, relatives, people of the same age group and to children. Sie is the formal way to address both one or more persons.

Subject pronouns

ich [ikh] *(I)*
du [doo] *(you [singular/familiar])*
er, sie, es [air, zee, es] *(he, she, it)*
wir [veer] *(we)*
ihr [eer] *(you [plural/familiar])*
sie [zee] *(they)*
Sie [zee] *(you [singular and plural/formal])*

Object pronouns (accusative/dative)

mich [mikh] *(me)*
mir [meer] *(to me)*
dich [dikh] *(you [singular/familiar])*
dir [deer] *(to you [singular/familiar])*
ihn [een] *(him)*
ihm [eem] *(to him, to it)*
sie [zee] *(her)*

ihr [eer] *(to her)*
es [es] *(it)*
uns [oons] *(us, to us)*
euch [oykh] *(you, to you [plural/familiar])*
sie [zee] (*them)*
ihnen [eenen] *(to them)*
Sie [zee] *(you [singular and plural/formal])*
Ihnen [eenen] *(to you [singular and plural/formal])*

Possessive pronouns

The possessive pronoun is declined in much the same way as the indefinite article. The ending depends on the gender, number and case of the noun it qualifies, e.g. Ich habe meine Bücher [ikh **hah**buh **miy**nuh **bew**kher] *(I have my books)*.

masculine:
Nom. mein [miyn] *(my)*
Acc. meinen [**miy**nen] *(my)*
Gen. meines [**miy**nes] *(my)*
Dat. meinem [**miy**nem] *(my)*

feminine:
Nom. meine [**miy**nuh] *(my)*
Acc. meine [**miy**nuh] *(my)*
Gen. meiner [**miy**ner] *(my)*
Dat. meiner [**miy**ner] *(my)*

neuter:
Nom. mein [miyn] *(my)*
Acc. mein [miyn] *(my)*
Gen. meines [**miy**nes] *(my)*
Dat. meinem [**miy**nem] *(my)*

plural for all genders:
Nom. meine [**miy**nuh] *(my)*
Acc. meinen [**miy**nen] *(my)*
Gen. meiner [**miy**ner] *(my)*
Dat. meinen [**miy**nen] *(my)*

The other possessive pronouns are declined in the same way:
dein [diyn] *(your [singular/familiar])*
sein [ziyn] *(his, its)*
ihr [eer] *(her, their)*
unser [**oon**zer] *(our)*
euer [**oy**er] *(your [plural/familiar])*
Ihr [eer] *(your [singular and plural/formal])*

Demonstrative pronouns

Dieser [**dee**zer] *(this)* is the nominative masculine singular form of the main demonstrative pronoun. It again is declined and its ending depends on the gender, number and case of the noun it qualifies.

Prepositions

Prepositions in German are used to indicate a number of different meanings, e.g. Ich wohne bei meinen Eltern [ikh **voh**nuh by **miy**nen **el**tern] *(I live with my parents);* Biegen Sie rechts bei den Verkehrsampeln ab [**bee**gen zee rekhts by dayn fair**kair**sampeln ap] *(Turn left at the lights).*

Prepositions govern one (or two) case(s). Some take the accusative, e.g. durch [doorkh] *(through)*, gegen [**gay**gen] *(against);* some take the dative, e.g. mit [mit] *(with)*, von [fon] *(of, from, by)*; some take the accusative or dative, e.g. in [in] *(in)*, auf [owf] *(on, on to)*; others take the genitive, e.g. während [**vair**ent] *(during)*, wegen [**vay**gen] *(because of)*.

Verbs

In German, verb endings change for all persons and in all tenses. Tense formation is either regular (weak) or irregular (strong). Two very important verbs are **sein** (irregular) and **haben** (regular). They are used to form the perfect tense.

sein [ziyn] *(to be)*
ich bin [ikh bin] *(I am)*
du bist [doo bist] *(you are [singular/familiar])*
er, sie, es ist [air, zee, es ist] *(he, she, it is)*
wir sind [veer zint] *(we are)*
ihr seid [eer ziyt] *(you are [plural/familiar])*
sie sind [zee zint] *(they are)*
Sie sind [zee zint] *(you are [singular and plural/formal])*

haben [**hah**ben] *(to have)*
ich habe [ikh **hah**buh] *(I have)*
du hast [doo hast] *(you have [singular/familiar])*
er, sie, es hat [air, zee, es hat] *(he, she, it has)*

wir haben [veer **hah**ben] *(we have)*
ihr habt [eer hapt] *(you have [plural/familiar])*
sie haben [zee **hah**ben] *(they have)*
Sie haben [zee **hah**ben] *(you have [singular and plural/formal])*

Weak verbs

Many verbs, known as "weak", are conjugated by changing their endings. In most cases the different tenses are formed according to a regular pattern.

Present tense:
ich mache [ikh **ma**khuh] *(I make/do)*
du machst [doo makhst] *(you make/do [singular/familiar])*
er, sie, es macht [air, zee, es makht] *(he, she it makes/does)*
wir machen [veer **ma**khen] *(we make/do)*
ihr macht [eer makht] *(you make/do [plural/familiar])*
sie machen [zee **ma**khen] *(they make/do)*
Sie machen [zee **ma**khen] *(you make/do [singular and plural/formal])*

Strong verbs

However, many verbs are "strong" verbs. Their form changes more drastically in both present and past tenses.

Present tense:
ich spreche [ikh **shpre**khuh] *(I speak)*
du sprichst [doo shprikhst] *(you speak [singular/familiar])*
er, sie, es spricht [air, zee, es shprikht] *(he, she, it speaks)*
wir sprechen [veer **shpre**khen] *(we speak)*
ihr sprecht [eer shprekht] *(you speak [plural/familiar])*
sie sprechen [zee **shpre**khen] *(they speak)*
Sie sprechen [zee **shpre**khen] *(you speak [singular and plural/formal])*

Modal verbs

Modal verbs are often used with another verb in the infinitive, e.g. Ich muss den Brief finden [Ikh moos dayn breef finden] *(I have to find the letter)*. The two most common of these are:

können [**ker**nen] *(to be able to)*
ich kann [ikh kan] *(I can)*
du kannst [doo kanst] *(you can [singular/familiar])*
er, sie, es kann [air, zee, es kan] *(he, she, it can)*
wir können [veer **ker**nen] *(we can)*
ihr könnt [eer kernt] *(you can [plural/familiar])*
sie können [zee **ker**nen] *(they can)*
Sie können [zee **ker**nen] *(you can [singular and plural/formal])*

müssen [**mew**sen] *(to have to)*
ich muss [ikh moos] *(I must)*
du musst [doo moost] *(you must [singular/familiar])*
er, sie es musst [air, zee, es moost] *(he, she, it must)*
wir müssen [veer **mew**sen] *(we must)*
ihr müsst [eer mewst] *(you must [plural/familiar])*
sie müssen [zee **mew**sen] *(they must)*
Sie müssen [zee **mew**sen] *(you must [singular and plural/formal])*

Perfect tense

The perfect tense is usually formed with the auxiliary verb haben *(to have)*, e.g. Ich habe meine Uhr verloren [ikh **hah**buh **miy**nuh oor fair**lo**ren] *(I have lost my watch)*. The past participle, in this case formed from the strong verb verlieren, always goes at the end of the sentence. When the verb indicates movement or a change of state, the perfect tense is formed with sein, e.g. Er ist gegangen [air ist ge**gang**en] *(He's gone)*.

Word order

In a sentence containing two or more adverbial phrases, the normal word order is: time, manner, place, e.g. Ich fahre morgen mit der Eisenbahn nach Frankfurt [ikh **fah**ruh **mor**gen mit dair **iy**zenbahn nakh **frank**furt] *(I am going by train to Frankfurt tomorrow)*.

Negatives

The negative is formed with nicht [nikht] *(not)*. It is generally placed before the word negated, e.g. Das ist nicht wahr [das ist nikht vahr] *(that is not true)*.

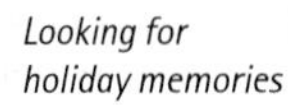
Looking for holiday memories

General

Hello and goodbye

Good morning.	Guten Morgen! [**goo**ten **mor**gen]
Hello./Good morning./Good afternoon.	Guten Tag! [**goo**ten tahg]
Good evening.	Guten Abend! [**goo**ten **ah**bent]
Good night.	Gute Nacht! [**goo**tuh nakht]
Hello.	Hallo! [huh**law**]
How's it going?	Wie geht's? [vee gayts]
How are you?	Wie geht es Ihnen/dir? [vee gayts **ee**nen/deer]
* Danke, gut. [**dan**kuh goot]	Fine, thank you.
And you?	Und Ihnen/dir? [unt **ee**nen/deer]
Goodbye.	Auf Wiedersehen! [owf **vee**derzayn]
Bye./See you.	Tschüs! [chews]
See you tomorrow.	Bis morgen. [bis **mor**gen]
Regards to the family.	Grüße an die Familie. [**grew**suh an dee fa**meel**yuh]
Thank you for everything.	Vielen Dank für alles. [**fee**len dank fewr **al**lus]
We really enjoyed it.	Es hat uns sehr gefallen. [es hat uns zair ge**fal**len]

Introducing yourself

Mr/Mrs/Miss ...	Herr/Frau/Fräulein [hair/frow/**froy**liyn]
What's your name?	Wie heißen Sie/heißt du? [vee **hiy**sen zee/hiyst doo]
My name is ...	Ich heiße ... [ikh **hiy**suh]

This is/These are	**Das ist/sind**[das ist/zint]
my husband/my boyfriend	mein Mann/mein Freund [miyn man/miyn froynt]
my wife/my girlfriend	meine Frau/meine Freundin [**miy**nuh frow/**miy**nuh **froyn**din]
my children.	meine Kinder. [**miy**nuh **kin**der]
Pleased to meet you.	Angenehm./Sehr erfreut. [**an**genaym/zair air**froyt**]
And you.	Gleichfalls. [**gliykh**fals]
Where are you from?	Woher kommen Sie/kommst du? [wo**hair** **kom**men zee/komst doo]
I'm/We're	**Ich bin/Wir sind** [ikh bin/veer zint]
from England	aus England [ows **eng**lant]
from the USA.	aus den USA. [ows dayn oo ess **ah**]

Communication

Do you speak English?	Sprechen Sie/Sprichst du Englisch? [**shpre**khen zee/shprikhst doo **eng**lish]
What's that called?	Wie heißt das? [vee hiysst das]
Pardon?/Sorry?	Wie bitte? [vee **bit**tuh]
What does that mean?	Was bedeutet das? [vas be**doy**tet das]
Did you understand that?	Haben Sie/Hast du verstanden? [**ha**ben zee/hast doo fair**shtan**den]
I don't understand.	Ich verstehe nicht. [ikh fair**shtay**uh nikht]
Could you speak more slowly, please?	Langsamer bitte! [**lang**zamer **bit**tuh]
Could you say that again, please?	Nochmal bitte! [**bit**tuh **nokh**mal]
Could you ... for me?	**Können Sie/Kannst du** [**ker**nen zee/kanst doo]
write that down	mir das aufschreiben [meer das **owf**shriyben]
explain that	mir das erklären [meer das air**klai**ren]
translate that	mir das übersetzen? [meer das ewber**zet**sen]

Civilities

Please.	Bitte. [**bit**tuh]
Thank you very much.	Vielen Dank. [**fee**len dank]
Thank you. The same to you.	Danke, gleichfalls. [**dan**kuh **gliykh**fals]

The formalities

Germany is a formal nation. In business and with acquaintances use **Herr** [hair] and **Frau** [frow] rather than calling people by their Christian names, unless they suggest otherwise. Peers of similar age and standing will usually be on first-name terms. Use **Sie** [zee] for "you" unless you are on very friendly terms.

People shake hands whenever they meet, and women are often pecked on both cheeks.

Thank you very much for all your trouble/help.	Danke für die Mühe/Hilfe. [**dan**kuh fewr dee **mew**uh/**hil**fuh]
* Bitte./Keine Ursache [**bi**tuh/**kiy**nuh **oor**zakhuh]	You're welcome./Don't mention it.
Sorry./Excuse me.	Entschuldigung!/Entschuldigen Sie mich.[ents**hool**digoong/ents**hool**digen zee mikh]
* Das macht nichts. [das makht nikhts]	It doesn't matter./Don't worry.
That's very nice of you.	Das ist sehr nett von Ihnen/dir. [das ist zair net fon **ee**nen]
I'm sorry about that.	Das tut mir Leid. [das toot meer liyt]
Welcome!	Herzlich willkommen! [**hair**tslikh vil**kom**men]
Congratulations!	Herzlichen Glückwunsch! [**hair**tslikhen **glewk**voonsh]
Happy birthday!	Alles Gute zum Geburtstag! [**al**lus **goo**tuh tsoom ge**boorts**tahg]
Have fun!	Viel Vergnügen! [feel fair**gnew**gen]
Get well soon!	Gute Besserung! [**goo**tuh **bes**seroong]
Good luck!	Viel Glück! [feel glewk]
Have a nice trip!	Gute Reise! [**goo**tuh **riy**zuh]
Merry Christmas!	Frohe Weihnachten! [**froh**uh **viy**nakhten]
Have a good holiday!	Schöne Ferien! [**sher**nuh **fair**yen]
Happy New Year!	Ein frohes neues Jahr! [iyn **froh**us **noy**us yahr]

Meeting people

Do you mind if I sit here?	Darf ich mich zu Ihnen/dir setzen? [darf ikh meekh tsoo **ee**nen/deer **zet**tsen]
Do you mind?	Gestatten Sie? [ges**htat**ten zee]
Are you	**Sind Sie/Bist du** [zint zee/bist doo]
(travelling) on you own	alleine (unterwegs) [a**liy**nuh (oonter**vaygs**)]
(travelling) with somebody	mit jemandem (unterwegs) [mit **yay**mandem (oonter**vaygs**)]
married?	verheiratet? [fair**hiy**rahtet]
Do you have a boyfriend/girlfriend?	Hast du einen Freund/eine Freundin? [hast doo **iy**nen froynt/ **iy**nuh **froyn**din]
How old are you?	Wie alt bist du? [vee alt bist doo]
I'm 25 years old.	Ich bin 25 Jahre alt. [ikh bin **fewnf**oont-tsvantsig **yah**ruh alt]
What do you do for a living?	Was sind Sie/bist du von Beruf? [vas zint zee/bist doo fon **buh**roof]
I'm	**Ich bin** [ikh bin]
still at school	Schüler(in) [**shew**ler(in)]
a student.	Student(in). [shtoo**dent**(in)]

Dialects

Hochdeutsch (High German) is spoken throughout the country, but cities and regions retain their own distinctive dialects. The Plattdeutsch (Low German) of Friesia is almost a language of its own. Some dialects, though part of the High German family, can be hard to understand even for native speakers. In Bavaria, for example, the question **Was wollen Sie** [vas **vo**len zee] *(what do you want?)* is spoken **Woss woin Sie** [vos voyn zee]. Dialects can vary considerably within a small area. Thus, for example, the Munich city dialect is very different to that spoken in nearby Rosenheim, though both are in Upper Bavaria. In Swabia they tend to pronounce the **ch** as **sh**, so **ich** [ikh] *(I)* becomes "**ish**", while in Franconia **t** and **p** are pronounced softly as **d** and **b**.

Can I buy you a drink?	Möchten Sie etwas trinken? [**mer**khten zee **et**vas **trin**ken]
Yes, thank you, good idea.	Ja, gerne, gute Idee. [ya **gair**nuh **goo**tuh ee**day**]
Why not?	Warum nicht? [va**rum** nikht]
No, thank you.	Nein, danke. [niyn **dan**kuh]
Perhaps another time.	Vielleicht ein andermal. [vee**liykht** iyn **an**dermal]
Do you like it here?	Gefällt es Ihnen/dir hier? [ge**felt** es **ee**nen/deer heer]
I like it very much here.	Mir gefällt es sehr gut. [meer ge**felt** es zair goot]
Is this your first time here?	Sind Sie/Bist du zum ersten Mal hier? [zint zee/bist doo tsoom **airs**ten mal heer]
No, I've been here before.	Nein, ich war schon einmal hier. [niyn ikh var shohn **iyn**mal heer]
Have you ever been to England?	Kennen Sie/kennst du England? [**ken**nen zee/kenst doo **eng**lant]
Come and visit me.	Besuchen Sie/Besuche mich doch einmal. [be**zoo**khen zee/be**zoo**khuh meekh dokh **iyn**mal]
Here's my address.	Hier ist meine Adresse. [heer ist **miy**nuh a**dres**suh]
How long have you been here?	Wie lange sind Sie/bist du schon hier? [vee **la**nguh zint zee/bist doo shohn heer]
For a week./For two days.	Seit einer Woche./Seit zwei Tagen. [ziyt **iy**ner **vo**khuh/ziyt tsviy **tah**gen]
How much longer are you staying?	Wie lange bleiben Sie/bleibst du noch hier? [vee **la**nguh **bliy**ben zee/**bliy**bst doo nokh]
Another week./Two days.	Noch eine Woche./Zwei Tage. [nokh **iy**nuh **vo**khuh/tsviy **tah**guh]
Shall we ... together today/tomorrow?	**Wollen wir heute/morgen zusammen** [**vol**len veer **hoy**tuh/**mor**gen tsoo**zam**en]
have dinner	zu Abend essen [tzoo **ah**bent essen]
go out	ausgehen [**ows**gayen]
go to the cinema/go dancing	ins Kino gehen/zum Tanzen gehen [ins **kee**no **gay**en/tsoom **tan**tsen **gay**en]
play tennis/go riding/go swimming?	Tennis spielen/reiten/schwimmen gehen? [**ten**nis **shpee**len/**riy**ten/**shvi**mmen **gay**en]

O.K., let's do that!	Einverstanden!/In Ordnung! [**iyn**fairstanden/in **ord**noong]
No, I don't want to.	Nein, ich möchte nicht. [niyn ikh **mer**khtuh nikht]
I can't, sorry.	Ich kann leider nicht. [ikh kan **liy**der nikht]
What time/Where shall we meet?	Wann/Wo treffen wir uns? [van/voh **tref**fen veer oons]
Shall I pick you up/take you home/take you to the bus stop?	Kann ich Sie/dich abholen/nach Hause bringen/zum Bus bringen? [kan ikh zee/deekh **ap**holen/nahkh **how**zuh **bri**ngen tsoom boos **bri**ngen]
No, that's not necessary.	Nein, das ist nicht nötig. [niyn das ist nikht **ner**tig]
It's been very nice.	Es war sehr schön. [es var zair shern]
When can we see each other again?	Wann treffen wir uns wieder? [van **tref**fen veer oons **vee**der]
I don't like that.	Das gefällt mir nicht. [das **ge**felt meer nikht]
I don't feel like it.	Dazu habe ich keine Lust. [**da**tsu **hah**buh ikh **kiy**nuh loost]
Leave me alone!	Lassen Sie mich in Ruhe! [**las**sen zee mikh in **roo**-uh]
Please go away!	Bitte gehen Sie! [**bit**tuh **gay**en zee]

Questions

What's that?	Was ist das? [vas ist das]
How much is that?	Was kostet das? [vas **kos**tet das]
Where is …?/can I get …?	Wo ist/gibt es …? [voh ist/gibt es]
Where does … go?	Wohin fährt …? [vo**hin** fairt]
What's that called?	Wie heißt das? [vee hiyst das]
How long does it last?	Wie lange dauert das? [vee **lan**guh **dow**ert das]
When does the concert start?	Wann beginnt das Konzert? [van be**gint** das kon**tsert**]
How far is it?	Wie weit ist das entfernt? [vee viyt ist das ent**fairnt**]
How long does it take?	Wie lange braucht man? [vee **lan**guh browkht man]

Could you — **Können Sie** [**ker**nen zee]
help me — mir helfen [meer **hel**fen]
show me, please? — mir das zeigen? [meer das **tsiy**gen]

Can I help you? — Kann ich Ihnen helfen? [kan ikh **ee**nen **hel**fen]

Interrogatives

What?/Who?	Was?/Wer? [vas/vair]
Which?	Welcher/Welche?/Welches? [**vel**kher/**vel**khuh/**vel**khes]
Where?/Where … to?	Wo?/Wohin? [voh/vo**hin**]
How?	Wie? [vee]
How much	Wie viel? [vee feel]
When?	Wann? [van]
How long?	Wie lange? [vee **lan**guh]
Why?	Warum? [va**room**]

Measurements

centimetre/metre/kilometre	Zentimeter/Meter/Kilometer [tsenti**may**ter/**may**ter/keelo**may**ter]
square metre/square kilometre/hectare	Quadratmeter/Quadratkilometer/Hektar [kwa**drat**mayter/kwa**drat**keelo**may**ter/hek**tahr**]
cubic metre	Kubikmeter [koo**bik**mayter]
kilometres per hour	Stundenkilometer (km/h) [**shtoon**denkeelo**may**ter]
a quarter of a litre	ein Viertelliter [iyn **feer**telleeter]
half a litre	ein halber Liter [iyn **hal**ber **lee**ter]
gram/half a kilo/kilogramme/ton	Gramm/Pfund/Kilo/Tonne [gram/pfoond/**kee**lo/**to**nnuh]
second/minute/hour	Sekunde/Minute/Stunde [se**koon**duh/mi**noo**tuh/**shtoon**duh]
day/week/month/year	Tag/Woche/Monat/Jahr [tahg/**vo**khuh/**moh**nat/yar]

Time

What's the (exact) time, please?	Wie spät ist es (genau), bitte? [vee shpayt ist es ge**now** **bit**tuh]
It's	**Es ist** [es ist]
1 o'clock/2 o'clock	ein Uhr/zwei Uhr [iyn oor/tsviy oor]
quarter past three	Viertel nach drei [**feer**tel nahkh driy]
quarter to five	Viertel vor fünf/drei viertel fünf [**feer**tel for fewnf/driy **feer**tel fewnf]
twenty past three (in the afternoon)	fünfzehn Uhr zwanzig [**fewnf**tsayn oor **tsvan**tsig]
half past three	halb vier [halb feer]
five to six	fünf Minuten vor sechs [fewnf mi**noo**ten for zekhs]
noon	zwölf Uhr mittags [tsverlf oor **mit**tahgs]
midnight.	Mitternacht. [**mit**ternakht]
What time do we have to be there?	Um wie viel Uhr müssen wir da sein? [um vee feel oor **mew**sen veer da ziyn]

Days of the week

Monday Montag [**mon**tahg]
Tuesday Dienstag [**deen**stahg]
Wednesday Mittwoch [**mit**vokh]
Thursday Donnerstag [**donn**erstahg]
Friday Freitag [**friy**tahg]
Saturday Samstag [**zam**stahg]
Sunday Sonntag [**zon**tahg]

Months

January Januar [**ya**noo-ar]
February Februar [**fe**broo-ar]
March März [merts]
April April [ah**pril**]
May Mai [miy]
June Juni [**yoo**nee]
July Juli [**yoo**lee]
August August [ow**goost**]
September September [zep**tem**ber]
October Oktober [ok**to**ber]
November November [no**vem**ber]
December Dezember [de**tsem**ber]

Seasons

spring Frühling [**frew**ling]
summer Sommer [**zo**mmer]
autumn Herbst [hairbst]
winter Winter [**vin**ter]

Around twelve./At twelve o'clock sharp. — Ungefähr/Pünktlich um zwölf Uhr. [oonge**fair**/**pewnkt**likh oom tsverlf oor]

When is breakfast/lunch/dinner? — Wann gibt es Frühstück/Mittag-/Abendessen? [van gibt es **frew**shtewk/**mit**tahg-/**ah**bentessen]

* Von acht bis neun Uhr. [fon akht bis noyn oor] — From 8 to 9.

Date

What's the date today? — Den Wievielten haben wir heute? [den **vee**feelten **hah**ben veer **hoy**tuh]

Today's the 1st/2nd/15th of August. — Heute ist der 1./2./15. August. [**hoy**tuh ist dair **airs**tuh/**tsviy**tuh/**fewnf**tsayntuh ow**goost**]

We'll arrive on the 20th of May. — Wir kommen am 20. Mai an. [veer **kom**men am **tsvan**tsigsten miy an]

We're staying until August 31st. — Wir bleiben bis zum 31. August. [veer **bliy**ben bis tsoom **iyn**oontdriyzigsten ow**goost**]

I was born on January 12th (1960). — Ich wurde am 12. Januar (neunzehnhundert sechzig) geboren. [ikh voorduh am **tsverl**ften **ya**noo-ar (**noyn**tsaynh**oon**dert **zekh**tsig) **ge**boren]

Indication of time

minute	Minute [mi**noo**tuh]
hour	Stunde [**shtoon**duh]
day	Tag [tahg]
week	Woche [**vo**khuh]
now	jetzt [yetst]
later	später [**shpayh**ter]
today	heute [**hoy**tuh]

yesterday	gestern [**ge**stairn]
this evening/tonight	heute Abend [**hoy**tuh **ah**bent]
tomorrow	morgen [**mor**gen]
tomorrow morning	morgen Vormittag [**mor**gen **for**mittahg]
tomorrow afternoon	morgen Nachmittag [**mor**gen **nakh**mittahg]
the day after tomorrow	übermorgen [**ew**bermorgen]
at the weekend	am Wochenende [am vokhen**en**duh]
in a fortnight	in 14 Tagen [in **feer**tsayn **tah**gen]
this year	dieses Jahr [**dee**zes yahr]
next year	nächstes Jahr [**naykh**stes yahr]
last year	voriges Jahr [**for**iges yahr]
every year	jedes Jahr [**yay**des yahr]
every day	täglich [**tayg**likh]
mornings	vormittags [**for**mittahgs]
at midday	mittags [**mit**tahgs]
afternoons	nachmittags [**nakh**mittahgs]
evenings	abends [**ah**bents]
at night	nachts [nakhts]
in time	rechtzeitig [**rekht**-tsiytig]
for a week (past continuous)	seit einer Woche [ziyt **iy**ner **vo**khuh]
from today	seit heute [ziyt **hoy**tuh]
(too) late	(zu) spät [tsoo shpeht]
two days ago	vor zwei Tagen [for tsviy **tah**gen]
before	vorher [**for**hair]
until tomorrow	bis morgen [bis **mor**gen]

Colours

I'm looking for a pair of blue/black trousers.	Ich suche eine blaue/schwarze Hose. [ikh **zoo**khuh **iy**nuh **blow**uh/**shvart**zuh **hoh**suh]
Do you have this shirt	**Haben Sie dieses Hemd** [**hah**ben zee **dee**zes hemd]
in white, too	auch in Weiß [owkh in viys]
in another colour?	in einer anderen Farbe? [in **iy**ner **an**deren **far**buh]
I don't like this colour.	Diese Farbe gefällt mir nicht. [**dee**zuh **far**buh ge**felt** meer nikht]

Colours and patterns

beige beige [baysh]
black schwarz [shvartz]
blue blau [blow]
brown braun [brown]
checked kariert [ka**reert**]
colourful bunt [boont]
dark dunkel [doonkel]
green grün [grewn]
grey grau [grow]
light hell [hell]
orange orange [or**onj**]
patterned gemustert [ge**moo**stert]
pink rosa [**roh**sa]
plain-coloured einfarbig [**iyn**farbig]
purple lila [**lee**la]
red rot [roht]
striped gestreift [ge**shtriyft**]
turquoise türkis [tewr**kees**]
white weiß [viys]
yellow gelb [gelb]

Weather

What a beautiful day!	Wie schön es heute ist! [vee shern es **hoy**tuh ist]
What a terrible day!	Wie abscheulich es heute ist! [vee ap**shoy**likh es **hoy**tuh ist]
Is it going to stay like this?	Wird es so bleiben? [veert es zo **bliy**ben]
What's the forecast?	Was sagt der Wetterbericht? [vas zagt dair **vet**terberikht]
It's going to be sunny.	Es wird sonnig. [es veert **zon**nikh]
It's going to get colder/ warmer.	Es wird kälter/wärmer. [es veert **kel**ter/**vair**mer]
It's hot/close/windy/stormy/ foggy.	Es ist heiß/schwül/windig/stürmisch/neblig. [es ist hiys/shvewl/**vin**dig/**shtewr**mish/**nay**blig]
It's going to rain/snow today/tomorrow.	Heute/Morgen soll es regnen/schneien. [**hoy**tuh/**mor**gen zol es **rayg**nen/**shniy**en]
When is it going to stop raining?	Wann hört es auf zu regnen? [van hert es owf tsoo **rayg**nen]
What's the temperature?	Wie viel Grad haben wir? [vee feel grahd **hah**ben veer]
It's 25 degrees Celsius (in the shade).	Fünfundzwanzig Grad Celsius (im Schatten). [**fewnf**oont-**tsvan**tsig grahd **tsel**seeoos (im **shat**ten)]
It's five degrees below zero.	Fünf Grad unter Null. [**fewnf** grahd **oon**ter nool]

Climate

Germany lies within the continental climate zone, which means it can be very hot in the summer and bitterly cold in the winter. You will, however, experience a slight change in climate when travelling from the northwest to the southeast. In the north around Hamburg, in Schleswig-Holstein and along the Baltic Sea the weather is more oceanic with milder winters and moderately warm summers. Further south it becomes more continental with greater variations.

The average temperature in the north is 0°C (32°F) in January and 17°C (63°F) in July. In the south temperature varies from -2°C (28°F) in January to 18°C (64°F) or even 20°C (68°F) in July. There can be cold periods in winter with temperatures falling to -10°C (14°F) or even -20°C (-4°F). In July and August temperatures can reach between 30°C (86°F) and 35°C (95°F), but periods of cold and rainy days in July and August are not uncommon either. So be prepared for any weather and bring along a sweater and an umbrella as well as clothing for warm, sunny days. Annual average rainfall varies between 750mm (30 inches) in the north and 620mm (26 inches) in the Rhine Valley. But there are places in Bavaria where rainfall is even higher and the Alps is by far the wettest region.

Southern Germany is affected by another climatic phenomenon known as the Föhn [fern]. This warm, dry wind blows down from the Alps into southern Bavaria and Swabia. The Föhn has two effects: it clears the sky so that it is possible to see the Alps even from Munich, but it can also cause headaches.

The best time to travel to Germany is between late May and early October. Skiers will find the best conditions between mid-December and March.

Routes in rural Thuringia

Getting Around

Customs formalities

* Ihren Pass! [**ee**ren pass]	Your passport!
* Ihren Führerschein! [**ee**ren **few**rershiyn]	Your driving licence!
* Ihre Fahrzeugpapiere! [**ee**ruh **fahr**-tsoygpa**pee**ruh]	Your vehicle documents!
* Wohin fahren Sie? [vo**hin fah**ren zee]	What's your destination?
I'm going to/We're going to ...	Ich fahre/Wir fahren nach ... [ihk **fahr**uh/veer **fahr**en nahkh]
I'm	**Ich bin** [ikh bin]
a tourist.	Tourist [too**rist**]
on a business trip.	auf Geschäftsreise. [owf ge**shefts**riysuh)
* Haben Sie ein Rückflugticket? [**hah**ben zee iyn **rewk**floogticket]	Do you have a return ticket?
* Haben Sie etwas zu verzollen? [**hah**ben zee **et**vas tsoo fair**tsol**len]	Do you have anything to declare?
No, I have	**Nein, ich habe** [niyn ikh **hah**buh]
nothing to declare	nichts zu verzollen [nikhts tsoo fair**tsol**len]
only a few presents.	nur einige Geschenke. [noor **iy**neeguh ge**shen**kuh]
Do I have to pay duty on this?	Muss ich das verzollen? [moos ikh das fair**tsol**len]

How many ... are duty-free?	**Wie viele ... sind zollfrei?** [vee **fee**luh zint tsol**friy**]
cigarettes	Zigaretten [tsiga**ret**ten]
litres of wine/spirits	Liter Wein/Spirituosen [**lee**ter viyn/shpiritoo-**o**sen]
Can I	**Kann ich** [kan ikh]
call the British embassy	mit der britischen Botschaft sprechen [mit dair **bri**tishen **boht**shaft **shpre**khen]
call my consulate?	mit meinem Konsulat sprechen? [mit **miy**nem konzoo**laht** **shpre**khen]

Asking directions

How do I get	**Wie komme ich** [vee **kom**muh ikh]
to ...	nach ... [nahkh]
onto the motorway	zur Autobahn [tsoor **ow**tobahn]
to the city centre	ins Zenrum [ins **tsen**troom]
to ... Street	zur ... Straße [tsoor **shtrah**suh]
to the station/bus station	zum Bahnhof/Busbahnhof [tsoom **bahn**hof/**boos**bahnhof]
to the airport/harbour?	zum Flughafen/Hafen? [tsoom **floog**hahfen/**hah**fen]
* An der Kreuzung [an dair **kroy**tsoong]	At the crossroads
* Nach der Ampel [nakh dair **am**pel]	After the traffic light
* Nach 500 Metern [nakh **fewnf**hoondert **may**tern]	After 500 metres
* rechts/links abbiegen [rekhts/links **ap**beegen]	turn right/left
* geradeaus fahren [ge**ra**duhows **fah**ren]	go straight ahead
* zurückfahren/zurückgehen. [tsoo**rewk**-**fah**ren/-**gay**en]	turn around/go back.
How far is it to ...?	Wie weit ist es nach ...? [vee viyt ist es nahkh]

Car, motorbike and bicycle hire

I'd like to hire	**Ich möchte ... mieten.** [ikh **mer**khtuh **mee**ten]
a car	ein Auto [iyn **ow**to]
a minibus	einen Kleinbus [**iy**nen **kliyn**boos]
a camper van	ein Wohnmobil [iyn **vohn**mobeel]
a motorbike	ein Motorrad [iyn mo**tor**-rahd]
a bicycle	ein Fahrrad [iyn **far**-rahd]
for two days	für 2 Tage [fewr tsviy **tah**guh]
from today/tomorrow	ab heute/morgen [ap **hoy**tuh/**mor**gen]
What do you charge	**Wie viel kostet das Fahrzeug** [vee feel **kos**tet das **fahr**tsoyg]
per day/week	pro Tag/Woche [pro tahg/**vo**khuh]
per kilometre?	pro Kilometer? [pro keelo**may**ter]

Is there a mileage charge?	Gibt es eine Kilometerbegrenzung? [gibt es **iy**nuh keelo**may**terbe**gren**tsoong]
How many kilometres are included in the price?	Wie viele Kilometer sind im Preis enthalten? [vee **fee**luh keelo**may**ter zint im priys ent**hal**ten]
Is the tank full?	Ist das Auto vollgetankt? [ist das **ow**to folge**tankt**]
What petrol does it take?	Welches Benzin muss ich tanken? [**vel**khes ben**tseen** moos ikh **tan**ken]
How much is the deposit?	Wie hoch ist die Kaution? [vee hokh ist dee kowts**yon**]
Does the vehicle have comprehensive insurance?	Ist das Auto vollkaskoversichert? [ist das **ow**to **fol**kaskofair**zi**khert]
Would I have to pay any excess?	Wie hoch ist die Selbstbeteiligung? [vee hokh ist dee **zelbst**betiyligoong]
Can I hand the car back in . . .?	Kann ich das Fahrzeug in . . . zurückgeben? [kan ikh das **fahr**tsoyg in tsoo**rewk**geben]
When do I have to be back by?	Bis wann muss ich das Fahrzeug zurückbringen? [bis van moos ikh das **fahr**tsoyg tsoo**rewk**bringen]

Parking

Can I park here?	Kann ich hier parken? [kan ikh heer **par**ken]
Is there a . . . near here?	**Gibt es hier** [gibt es heer]
a (supervised) car park	einen (bewachten) Parkplatz [**iy**nen (be**vakh**ten) **park**plats]
a multi-storey car park/ a garage	ein Parkhaus/eine Garage? [iyn **park**hows/**iy**nuh ga**rah**shuh]
Is the car park open all night?	Ist das Parkhaus nachts geöffnet? [ist das **park**hows nakhts ge-**er**fnet]
* Belegt. [be**laygt**]	Full.
How much is it	**Wie viel kostet es** [vee feel **kos**tet es]
per hour	pro Stunde [pro **shtoon**duh]
per day?	pro Tag? [pro tahg]

Traffic signs

Achtung! caution
Ausfahrt freihalten! keep clear
Autobahn motorway
Baustelle road works
Einbahnstraße one-way street
Gefahr! danger
Gefährliche Kurve! dangerous bend
Langsamer fahren! reduce speed
Parkhaus car park
Parkverbot no parking
Radweg cycle path
Rechts (Links) fahren! keep right (left)
Sackgasse dead end
Scheinwerfer einschalten! use your headlights
Stau traffic jam
Überholverbot no overtaking
Umgehungsstraße bypass
Umleitung diversion
Vorfahrt beachten! give way

Getting around by road

Germany is criss-crossed by a network of motorways or **Autobahnen** [ow-tobahnen], extending over 14,000 km (8,700 miles). There is no toll and there are **Raststätten** [rast-**shtet**ten] *(service stations)* every 30 to 50 km (20 to 30 miles) to provide refreshments.

The general speed limit in Germany is 50 kmph (31mph) in towns and villages and 100 kmph (62 mph) on open roads. Motorways and dual carriageways have a recommended speed limit of 130 kmph (81 mph), but you will still see drivers overtaking at 180 kmph or more.

Petrol

Where's the nearest petrol station, please? — Wo ist bitte die nächste Tankstelle? [voh ist **bit**tuh dee **naykh**stuh **tank**shtelluh]

Fill up, please./20 litres of . . . , please. — **Bitte volltanken./20 Liter . . . , bitte.** [**bi**tuh **fol**tanken/**tsvan**tsig **lee**ter **bi**tuh]
- unleaded — Normal bleifrei [nor**mal bliy**friy]
- super unleaded — Super bleifrei [**zoo**per]
- four-star — Super verbleit [**zoo**per fair**bliyt**]
- diesel — Diesel [**dee**zel]

Please check — **Bitte prüfen Sie** [**bit**tuh **prew**fen zee]
- the oil — den Ölstand [den **erl**shtand]
- the tyre pressure — den Reifendruck [den **riy**fendrook]
- the water. — das Kühlwasser. [das **kewl**vasser]

Breakdown and accident

My car's broken down. — Ich habe eine Panne. [ikh **hah**buh **iy**nuh **pan**nuh]

I've had an accident. — Ich habe einen Unfall gehabt [ikh **hah**buh **iy**nen oonfal ge**hapt**]

Could you give me a lift — **Bitte nehmen Sie mich mit** [**bi**tuh **nay**men zee mikh mit]
- to the nearest petrol station/garage — zur nächsten Tankstelle/Werkstatt? [tsoor **naykh**sten **tank**shtelluh/**vairk**shtat]

Could you — **Können Sie** [**ker**nen zee]
- tow my car away — mich abschleppen [mikh **ap**shleppen]
- help me — mir helfen [meer **hel**fen]
- help me jump-start my car — mir Starthilfe geben [meer **shtart**heelfuh **gay**ben]
- lend me your jack — mir Ihren Wagenheber leihen [meer **ee**ren **vah**genheber **liy**en]
- send me a breakdown truck — den Pannendienst benachrichtigen [den **pan**nendeenst be**nahkh**rikhtigen]
- call the police/fire brigade — die Polizei/Feuerwehr rufen [dee polit**siy**/foyer**vair roo**fen]
- call an ambulance/doctor? — einen Krankenwagen/Arzt rufen? [**iy**nen **krank**en**vah**gen/artst **roo**fen]

Are you injured?
Sind Sie verletzt? [zeent zee fair**letst**]

Nobody is injured.
Es ist niemand verletzt. [es ist **nee**mand fair**letst**]

Somebody is (seriously) injured.
Es ist jemand (schwer) verletzt.
[es ist **yay**mand (shvair) fair**letst**]

Give me . . ., please.
Geben Sie mir bitte [**gay**ben zee meer **bit**tuh]

your name and address
Ihren Namen und Ihre Anschrift
[**ee**ren **nah**men oont **ee**ruh **an**shrift]

your insurance number
Ihre Versicherungsnummer.
[**ee**ruh fair**zi**kheroongsnoomer]

I was/You were/He was
Ich bin/Sie sind/Er ist [ikh bin/zee zint/air ist]

driving too fast
zu schnell gefahren [tsoo shnel ge**fahr**en]

driving too close.
zu dicht aufgefahren. [tsoo deekht owfge**fahr**en]

I/You/He
Ich habe/Sie haben/Er hat
[ikh **hah**buh/zee **hah**ben/air hat]

ignored the right of way
die Vorfahrt missachtet [dee **for**fahrt miss**akh**tet]

went through a red light.
das Rotlicht übersehen.
[das **roht**likht ewber**zay**en]

Did you witness the accident?
Sind Sie Zeuge des Unfalls?
[zint zee **tsoy**guh des **oon**fals]

Garage

Where's the nearest (Vauxhall) garage?
Gibt es hier eine (Opel-)Werkstatt?
[gibt es heer **iy**nuh (**o**pel) **vairk**shtat]

The engine
Der Motor [dair mo**tor**]

won't start
springt nicht an [shpringt nikht an]

is losing oil
verliert Öl [fair**leert** erl]

doesn't work.
funktioniert nicht. [foonktsyo**neert** nikht]

The brakes don't work.
Die Bremsen sind nicht in Ordnung.
[dee **brem**zen zint nikht in **ord**noong]

Car, motorbike, bicycle

battery	Batterie [batte**ree**]
brake	Bremse [**brem**zuh]
bicycle tyre	Fahrradreifen [far-rahd**riy**fen]
bicycle helmet	Fahrradhelm [far-rahd**helm**]
car key	Autoschlüssel [owto**shlew**sel]
catalytic converter	Katalysator [katali**za**tor]
chain	Fahrradkette [far-rahd**ke**tuh]
child seat	Kindersitz [kinder**zits**]
clutch	Kupplung [**koop**loong]
engine	Motor [mo**tor**]
exhaust	Auspuff [**ows**poof]
fan belt	Keilriemen [**kiyl**reemen]
first-aid kit	Verbandskasten [fair**bants**kasten]
fuse	Sicherung [**zi**kheroong]
(1st/2nd/3rd/4th/5th) gear	(erster/zweiter/dritter/vierter/fünfter) Gang [(**air**ster/**tsviy**ter/**dri**tter/**feer**ter/**fewnf**ter) gang]
gearshift	Gangschaltung [**gang**shaltoong]
hand brake	Handbremse [**hand**bremzuh]
headlights	Scheinwerfer [**shiyn**vairfer]
helmet	Motorradhelm [motor-rahd**helm**]
horn	Hupe [**hoo**puh]
ignition cable	Zündkabel [**tsewnt**kahbel]
light bulb	Glühbirne [**glew**beernuh]
pump	Luftpumpe [looft**poom**puh]
puncture repair kit	Flickzeug [**flik**tsoyg]
radiator	Kühler [**kew**ler]
rear light	Rücklicht [**rewk**likht]
reverse gear	Rückwärtsgang [**rewk**vairtsgang]
screw	Schraube [**shrow**buh]
screwdriver	Schraubenzieher [**shrow**bentsee-er]
seat belt	Sicherheitsgurt [**zi**kherhiytsgoort]
spare part	Ersatzteil [air**zats**tiyl]
spare tyre	Reserverad [ruh**zair**vuhrahd]
spark plugs	Zündkerzen [**tsewnt**kairtsen]
starter	Starter [**shtar**ter]
steering	Lenkung [**len**koong]
tank	Tank [tank]
tools	Werkzeug [**vairk**tsoyg]
tow rope	Abschleppseil [**ap**shlepziyl]
tube	Schlauch [shlowkh]
tyre	Reifen [**riy**fen]
windscreen wipers	Scheibenwischer [**shiy**benvisher]
warning triangle	Warndreieck [**varn**driyek]

The warning light is on.	Die Kontrolllampe leuchtet. [dee kon**trol**-lampuh **loykh**tet]
The exhaust/radiator is leaking/is faulty.	Der Auspuff/Kühler ist undicht/defekt. [dair **ows**poof/**kew**ler ist oon**dikht**/de**fekt**]
How much will the repairs be?	Was wird es kosten? [vas veert es **kos**ten]
When will the car be ready?	Wann ist der Wagen fertig? [van ist dair **vah**gen **fair**tig]

Hitchhiking

Are you going to ...?	Fahren Sie nach ...? [**fahr**en zee nahkh]
Could you give me a lift?	Können Sie mich mitnehmen? [**ker**nen zee mekh **mit**naymen]
I'd like to get out here, please!	Ich möchte hier bitte aussteigen!. [ikh **merk**htuh heer **bit**tuh **ows**-shtiygen]
Thanks for the lift!	Danke fürs Mitnehmen. [**dan**kuh fewrs **mit**naymen]

Getting around by train and bus

Where's the station/bus station, please?	Wo ist der Bahnhof/Busbahnhof, bitte? [voh ist dair **bahn**hof/**boos**bahnhof **bit**tuh]
When's the next train/bus to ...?	Wann fährt ein Zug/Bus nach ...? [van fert iyn tsoog/boos nahkh]
Do I have to change?	Muss ich umsteigen? [moos ikh **oom**shtiygen]
Which platform does the train leave from?	Von welchem Gleis fährt der Zug ab? [von **vel**khem gliys fert dair tsoog ap]
When does the train/bus arrive in ...?	Wann kommt der Zug in ... an? [van komt dair tsoog in an]
Is there a connection to ... in ...?	Habe ich Anschluss nach ... in ...? [**hah**buh ikh **an**shloos nahkh in]
How much is it to ...?	Was kostet die Fahrt nach ...? [vas **kos**tet dee fahrt nahkh]
Are there special rates for children?	Gibt es eine Ermäßigung für Kinder? [gibt es **iy**ne air**may**sigoong fewr **kin**der]
A ... ticket/2 ... tickets to ..., please.	**Einmal .../Zweimal ... nach ..., bitte.** [**iyn**mal **tsviy**mal nahkh **bit**tuh]
single/return/first/second-class.	einfach/hin und zurück/erster/zweiter Klasse [**iyn**fakh/hin oont tsoo**rewk**/**air**ster/**tsviy**ter **klas**suh]
2 adults and 2 children to ..., please.	2 Erwachsene und 2 Kinder nach ..., bitte. [tsviy air**vakh**senuh oont tsviy **kin**der nahkh **bit**tuh]
I'd like to book ... on the 2 o'clock train/bus to ...	**Bitte reservieren Sie ... für den Zug/Bus um 14 Uhr nach ...** [**bit**tuh resair**vee**ren zee fewr den tsoog/boos oom **feer**tsayn oor nahkh]
a (window) seat	einen (Fenster) Platz [**iy**nen (**fen**ster) plats]
a non-smoker/smoker seat	einen Nichtraucher-/Raucherplatz [**iy**nen **nikht**rowkher/**row**kher plats]
a couchette/sleeper	einen Liegewagenplatz/Schlafwagenplatz [**iy**nen **lee**guhvahgenplats/**shlahf**vahgenplats]

I'd like to take my bicycle with me.	Ich möchte mein Fahrrad mitnehmen. [ikh **mer**khtuh miyn **fahr**-rad **mit**naymen]
Where can I find . . ., please?	**Wo finde ich bitte** [voh **fin**duh ikh]
the information desk	den Informationsschalter [den informats**yon**shalter]
the left-luggage office	die Gepäckaufbewahrung [dee ge**pek**owfbevahroong]
the lockers	die Schließfächer? [dee **shlees**fekher]
Is this the train/bus to . . .?	Ist das der Zug/Bus nach . . .? [ist das dair tsoog/boos nahkh]
Is this seat taken, please?	Ist dieser Platz besetzt? [ist **dee**zer plats **be**zetst]
Excuse me, that's my seat.	Entschuldigung, das ist mein Platz. [ent**shool**digoong das ist miyn plats]

Getting around by plane

I'd like	**Ich möchte** [ikh **merkh**tuh]
to book a flight to . . . on . . .	einen Flug buchen nach . . . am . . . [**iy**nen floog **boo**khen nahkh am]
one-way/return	einfach/Hin- und Rückflug [**iyn**fakh/hin- oont **rewk**floog]
economy class/business class/first class	Touristenklasse/Businessklasse/1. Klasse [too**ris**ten**klas**suh/**bis**nesklassuh/**air**ster **klas**suh]
for 1 person/4 people	für eine Person/4 Personen [fewr **iy**nuh pair**sohn**/feer pair**sohn**en]
to confirm a return flight	einen Flug rückbestätigen [**iy**nen floog **rewk**bestaytigen]
to cancel the flight/change the booking.	den Flug stornieren/umbuchen. [dayn floog shtor**nee**ren/**oom**bookhen]

Trains, buses and trams

Trains in Germany are comfortable and almost always on time. Trains range from the ultra-fast ICE (Inter City Express) through to slow regional trains. A variety of discounts and passes is available, particularly for weekend travel. **Europabusse** [oy**ro**pabusuh] are a cheap way of travelling between cities, many departing from railway stations. **Bahnbusse** [**bahn**busuh] *(buses owned by German Railways)* operate services that link towns with smaller villages in the country. In remote parts this is usually the only form of transport. Among the different coach tour companies, **Europa Bus Dienst** [oy**ro**pa boos deenst] *(European Bus Service)*, run by Deutsche Touring GmbH, offer scenic itineraries designed primarily for tourists.

Every large city has good public transport with highly efficient bus services. You usually buy the bus ticket from the driver or at coin-operated machines on the bus or at the bus stop. In large cities such as Berlin, Hamburg, Cologne, Munich, Frankfurt and Stuttgart, the bus routes are integrated with the **Straßenbahn** [**shtra**senbahn] *(tram), the* **U-Bahn** [**oo**bahn] *(underground)*, and the **S-Bahn** [**ess**bahn] *(above-ground suburban railway)*. The same ticket may be used on all four means of transport.

Signs

Ausgang exit
Auskunft information
Bahnsteig/Gleis platform
Besetzt occupied
Frei vacant
Kein Trinkwasser not for drinking
Liegewagen couchette car
Notbremse communication cord
Schlafwagen sleeping car/sleeper
Speisewagen dining car
Toiletten/WC toilets
Waschraum washroom

Where's — **Wo ist** [voh ist]
Terminal 1/2/3 — Terminal 1/2/3 [**ter**minal iyns/tsviy/driy]
Gate A/B/C/D — Ausgang A/B/C/D [**ows**gang ah/bay/tsay/day]
the Lufthansa desk — der Lufthansa-Schalter [dair **loof**thansa **shal**ter]
the information desk? — der Informationsschalter? [dair informat**syons**-shalter]

When does the plane from … arrive? — Wann landet die Maschine aus …? [van **lan**det dee ma**shee**nuh ows]

Are there any … seats left? — **Sind noch Plätze frei** [zint nokh **ple**tsuh friy]
window/aisle — am Fenster/am Gang [am **fen**ster/am gang]
smoking/non-smoking — für Raucher/Nichtraucher? [fewr **row**kher/**nikh**trowkher]

* Der Flug ist leider ausgebucht. [dair floog ist **liy**der **ows**gebookht] — The flight is full, I'm afraid.

How much is the ticket? — Wie viel kostet der Flug? [vee feel **kos**tet dair floog]
Are there any special rates/stand-by seats? — Gibt es Sondertarife/Stand-by-Plätze? [gibt es **zon**dertareef/**stand**-by-pletsuh]
When do I have to be at the airport? — Wann muss ich am Flughafen sein? [van moos ikh am **floog**hahfen ziyn]
How much is the airport tax? — Wie hoch ist die Flughafengebühr? [vee hokh ist dee **floog**hahfengebewr]

My suitcase/My bag — **Mein Koffer/meine Tasche** [miyn **ko**fer/**miy**nuh **ta**shuh]
has been damaged — ist beschädigt [ist be**shay**digt]
is missing. — ist verschwunden. [ist fair**shvoon**den]

Getting around by boat

When does the next ship/ferry leave for …? — Wann fährt ein Schiff/eine Fähre nach …? [van fert iyn shif/**iy**nuh **fair**uh nahkh]

* Das Schiff ist leider ausgebucht. [das shif ist **liy**der **ows**gebookht] — I'm afraid the ship is full.

How long does the crossing take? — Wie lange dauert die Überfahrt? [vee **lan**guh **dow**ert dee **ew**berfahrt]

I'd like	**Ich möchte** [ikh **mer**khtuh]
a ticket to ...	eine Schiffskarte nach ... [**iy**nuh **shifs**kartuh nahkh]
first class/tourist class	erster Klasse/zweiter Klasse [**air**ster **klas**suh/**tsviy**ter **klas**suh]
reclining seats	Liegesitze [**lee**guhsitsuh]
a single cabin	eine Einzelkabine [**iy**nuh **iyn**tselkabeenuh]
a double cabin	eine Zweibettkabine [**iy**nuh **tsvy**betkabeenuh]
an outside/inside cabin.	eine Außen-/Innenkabine. [**iy**nuh **ow**sen-/**in**nenkabeenuh]

I'd like to take the car with me.	Ich möchte mein Auto mitnehmen. [ikh **merkh**tuh miyn **ow**to **mit**naymen]
When do I/we have to be on board?	Wann muss ich/müssen wir an Bord sein? [van moos ikh/**mew**sen veer an bort ziyn]
When do we arrive at ...?	Wann legen wir in ... an? [van **lay**gen veer in an]
How long are we stopping?	Wie lange haben wir Aufenthalt? [vee **lan**guh **hah**ben veer **ow**fenhalt]

I'm looking for	**Ich suche** [ikh **zoo**khuh]
cabin number...	die Kabine Nummer ... [dee ka**bee**nuh **noo**mer]
the restaurant	das Restaurant [das resto**rant**]
the toilets	die Toiletten [dee toi**let**ten]
the promenade deck	das Promenadendeck [das prome**na**dendek]
the parking deck.	das Parkdeck. [das **park**dek]

Public transport

Bus, tram and underground

Is there a bus to ...?	Gibt es einen Bus nach ...? [gibt es **iy**nen boos nahkh]
How long does it take?	Wie lange dauert die Fahrt? [vee **lan**guh **dow**ert dee fahrt]

Excuse me, where's the nearest	**Wo ist bitte die nächste** [voh ist **bit**tuh dee **naykh**stuh]
bus stop	Bushaltestelle [**boos**haltuhshtelluh]
tram stop	Straßenbahnhaltestelle [**shtrah**senbahnhaltuhstelluh]
tube station?	U-Bahn Station? [**oo**bahn shtat**syon**]

... goes to ...?	**... fährt nach ...?** [fairt nahkh]
Which bus	Welcher Bus [**vel**kher boos]
Which tram	Welche Straßenbahn [**vel**khuh **shtra**senbahn]
Which (tube) train	Welche U-Bahn [**vel**khuh **oo**bahn]
When does the last bus leave?	Wann fährt der letzte Bus zurück? [van fairt dair **le**tstuh boos tsoo**rewk**]
How many stops is it?	Wie viele Haltestellen sind es? [vee **fee**luh **hal**tuhshtellen zint es]
Does this bus go to ...?	Ist dies der Bus nach ...? [ist dees dair boos nahkh]

Where do I have to	**Wo muss ich** [moos ikh]
get off	aussteigen [**ows**-shtiygen]
change for ...	umsteigen nach ... [**oom**shtiygen nahkh]
change	umsteigen [**oom**shtiygen]
to get to the station	zum Bahnhof [tsoom **bahn**hof]
to get to the airport	zum Flughafen [tsoom **floog**hahfen]
to get to the ... Hotel	zum Hotel ... [tsoom ho**tel**]
to get to the city centre?	ins Zentrum? [ins **tsen**troom]
Could you tell me when I have to get off, please.	Könnten Sie mir bitte sagen, wann ich aussteigen muss? [**ker**nten zee meer **bit**tuh **za**gen van ikh **ows**-shtiygen moos]
Where can I buy a ticket?	Wo kann ich einen Fahrschein kaufen? [voh kan ikh **iy**nen **fahr**shiyn **kow**fen]
A ticket to ... please.	Einen Fahrschein nach ..., bitte. [**iy**nen **fahr**shiyn nahkh **bit**tuh]
Are there day tickets?	Gibt es eine Tageskarte? [gibt es **iy**nuh **tah**geskartuh]
How much is a ticket to ...?	Wie viel kostet die Fahrt nach ...? [vee feel **kos**tet dee fahrt nahkh]
Could you stop here, please.	Könnten Sie bitte hier halten! [**ker**nten zee **bit**tuh heer **hal**ten]

Taxi

Could you call a taxi for me, please.	Könnten Sie mir bitte ein Taxi rufen [**ker**nten zee meer **bit**tuh iyn taxi **roo**fen]
Where's the nearest taxi rank?	Wo ist der nächste Taxistand? [voh ist dair **naykh**stuh **ta**xishtand]
Can you take me ..., please?	**Fahren Sie mich bitte** [**fahr**en zee mikh **bit**tuh]
to the station	zum Bahnhof [tsoom **bahn**hof]
to the ... Hotel	zum Hotel ... [tsoom ho**tel**]
to the airport	zum Flughafen [tsoom **floog**hahfen]
to the centre of town	in die Innenstadt [in dee **in**nenshtat]
to ...	nach ... [nahkh]
How much is it to (the) ...?	Was kostet die Fahrt nach/zum/zur...? [vas **kos**tet dee fahrt nahkh/tsoom/tsoor]
Could you stop here, please.	Halten Sie hier bitte. [**hal**ten zee **bit**tuh heer]
That's for you.	Das ist für Sie! [das ist fewr zee]
Keep the change.	Stimmt so! [shtimt zo]

Car sharing

In every major city there are **Mitfahrzentralen [mit**fahrtsen**trah**len] *(car sharing agencies, see Yellow Pages).* These arrange lifts to all European cities, plus trips throughout Germany. Driver and passenger share costs (the agencies suggest reasonable amounts) with the agency charging a fee. A few **Frauenmitfahrerzentralen** *(women-only agencies)* now operate.

The Bayerischer Hof, a famous landmark in Munich

Accommodation

Hotel and guesthouse

Where can I find	**Gibt es hier** [gibt es heer]
a good/cheap hotel	ein gutes/billiges Hotel [iyn **goo**tes/**bi**liges ho**tel**]
a guesthouse	eine Pension [**iy**nuh pens**yon**]
a bed and breakfast place	eine Privatunterkunft [**iy**nuh pri**vaht**oonterkoonft]
in the centre of town	zentral gelegen [tsent**ral** ge**lay**gen]
in a quiet location?	in ruhiger Lage? [in **roo**iger **la**guh]
Where is the ... Hotel?	Wo ist das Hotel ...? [voh ist das ho**tel**]

At the reception desk

I have a reservation.	Ich habe ein Zimmer reserviert. [ikh **hah**buh iyn **tsim**mer resair**veert**]
My name is ...	Mein Name ist ... [miyn **nah**muh ist]
Have you got any vacancies	**Haben Sie ein Zimmer frei** [**hah**ben zee iyn **tsi**mmer friy]
for 1 night	für eine Nacht [fewr **iy**nuh nakht]
for 1 day/2 days	für einen Tag/zwei Tage [fewr **iy**nen tahg/tsviy **tah**guh]
for 1 week/2 weeks?	für eine Woche/zwei Wochen? [fewr **iy**nuh **vo**khuh/tsviy **vo**khen]
* Wir sind leider ausgebucht. [veer zint **liy**der **ows**gebookht]	I'm afraid we're fully booked.
* Ab ... wird wieder etwas frei. [ab veert **vee**der etvas friy]	There's a vacancy from ...

I'd like/We'd like	**Ich möchte/Wir möchten** [ikh **mer**khtuh/veer **mer**khten]
a room with a shower	ein Zimmer mit Dusche [iyn **tsi**mmer mit **doo**shuh]
a single room	ein Einzelzimmer [iyn **iyn**tseltsimmer]
a double room	ein Doppelzimmer [iyn **dop**peltsimmer]
a room with twin beds	ein Zweibettzimmer [iyn **tsvi**ybet-tsimmer]
with a bath and toilet	mit Bad und Toilette [mit baht oont toi**let**tuh]
at the front/at the back.	zur Straße/zum Hof. [tsoor **shtrah**suh/tsoom hohf]
How much is the room	**Wie viel kostet das Zimmer** [vee feel **kos**tet das **tsi**mmer]
per person	pro Person [pro pair**sohn**]
per night/per week	pro Nacht/pro Woche [pro nakht/pro **vo**khuh]
with/without breakfast	mit/ohne Frühstück [mit/**oh**nuh **frew**shtewk]
with half board	mit Halbpension [mit halbpens**yon**]
with full board	mit Vollpension [mit follpens**yon**]
for children?	für Kinder? [fewr **kin**der]
Does the room have a television/telephone?	Ist das Zimmer mit Fernseher/Telefon? [ist das **tsi**mmer mit **fairn**zayer/**te**lefon]
I'd like to see the room.	Ich möchte das Zimmer sehen. [ikh **merkh**tuh das **tsi**mmer **zay**en]
This room is nice.	Dieses Zimmer ist schön. [**dee**zes **tsi**mmer ist shern]
I don't like this room.	Dieses Zimmer gefällt mir nicht. [**dee**zes **tsi**mmer ge**felt** meer nikht]
Do you have another room?	Haben Sie ein anderes Zimmer? [**hah**ben zee iyn **an**deres **tsi**mmer]
Can I pay by cheque/credit card?	Kann ich mit Scheck/Kreditkarte bezahlen? [kan ikh mit shek/kre**dit**kartuh be**tsah**len]
Do you have	**Haben Sie** [**hah**ben zee]
a car park	einen Parkplatz [**iy**nen **park**plats]
a swimming pool?	ein Schwimmbad? [iyn **shvim**baht]
Where is	**Wo ist** [voh ist]
the dining room?	der Speisesaal? [dair **shpiy**suhsahl]

Choosing a hotel

Most international chains have hotels in Germany that can easily be booked in advance. An increasing number of people offer overnight accommodation in their own houses. Look out for **Fremdenzimmer** [**frem**dentsimmer] or **Zimmer frei** [**tsi**mmer friy] signs.

Letting agencies or **Zimmervermittlung** [**tsi**mmerfairmittloong] charge a booking fee. Bed and breakfast hotels are often called **Pension** [pens**yon**] or **Privatquartier** [priv**aht**kwateer]. Their addresses can be obtained from the local tourist offices. Then you have the traditional **Gasthof** [**gast**hohf], usually located in the town centres. These range from old and simple (in other words, no en suite bathroom) to old and fully renovated. You'll also find modern hotels offering all the latest comforts. In rural areas many castles have been converted into luxury hotels.

What time is	**Um wie viel Uhr gibt es** [oom vee feel oor gipt es]
breakfast	Frühstück [**frew**shtewk]
lunch	Mittagessen [**mit**tahgessen]
dinner?	Abendessen? [**ah**bentessen]

▶ **(Food and Drink, see page 40)**

Would you wake me tomorrow at 7, please.	Könnten Sie mich bitte morgen um 7 Uhr wecken? [**ker**nten zee mikh **bit**tuh **mor**gen oom **zee**ben oor **vek**ken]
My key, please.	Meinen Schlüssel, bitte. [**miy**nen **shlew**sel **bit**tuh]
Room number 10, please.	Zimmer Nummer zehn, bitte. [**tsi**mmer **noom**er tsayn **bit**tuh]

Where can I	**Wo kann ich** [voh kan ikh]
change money	Geld umtauschen [geld **oom**towshen]
cash traveller's cheques	Reiseschecks einlösen [**riy**zuhsheks iyn**ler**sen]
buy stamps/postcards	Briefmarken/Postkarten kaufen [**breef**marken/**post**karten **kow**fen]
post this letter	diesen Brief einwerfen [**dee**zen breef **iyn**vairfen]
make a phone call?	telefonieren? [telefo**nee**ren]

Can I make a phone call to England from my room?	Kann ich von meinem Zimmer nach England telefononieren? [kan ikh fon **miy**nem **tsi**mmer nahkh **eng**lant telefo**nee**ren]
Please put me through to the number …	Verbinden Sie mich bitte mit der Nummer …! [fair**bin**den zee mikh **bit**tuh mit dair **noom**er]
Are there any letters/messages for me?	Gibt es Post/Nachrichten für mich? [gibt es post/**nahkh**rikhten fewr mikh]

Complaints

The room is dirty/too loud.	Das Zimmer ist schmutzig/zu laut. [das **tsi**mmer ist **shmoo**tsig/tsoo lowt]
There's no (hot) water.	Wir haben kein (warmes) Wasser. [veer **hah**ben kiyn (**var**mes) **va**sser]

… does not work.	**… funktioniert nicht.** [foonktsyo**neert** nikht]
The light	Das Licht [das likht]
The shower	Die Dusche [dee **doo**shuh]
The heating	Die Heizung [dee **hiy**tsoong]
The toilet won't flush.	Die Toilettenspülung funktioniert nicht. [dee toi**let**tenshpewloong foonktsyo**neert** nikht]

There are no	**Es fehlen** [es **fay**len]
towels	Handtücher [**hand**tewkher]
hangers.	Kleiderbügel. [**kliy**derbewgel]
There is no toilet paper.	Es fehlt Toilettenpapier. [es faylt toi**let**tenpapeer]

Could we have	**Wir brauchen noch** [veer **brow**khen nokh]
an extra blanket	eine Decke [**iy**nuh **dek**kuh]
an extra pillow.	ein Kopfkissen. [iyn **kopf**kissen]

Hotel Reservation by Fax

Hotel Ambassador	Hotel Ambassador
London	London
FAX ...	FAX ...
Dear Sir or Madam,	Sehr geehrte Damen und Herren,
I/We would like to book a single/double room from August 1 to 15, 2001. Ideally, the room should have a shower and a balcony. Please give me/us your prices for single/double rooms with breakfast/half board and confirm the reservation as soon as possible.	ich möchte/wir möchten vom 1. bis 15. August 2001 ein Zimmer für 1/2 Personen reservieren, wenn möglich mit Dusche und Balkon. Bitte teilen Sie mir/uns die Preise für Einzel-/Doppelzimmer mit Frühstück/Halbpension mit, und benachrichtigen Sie mich/uns umgehend über die erfolgte Buchung.
Yours sincerely	Mit freundlichen Grüßen

I've lost the key to my room. — Ich habe meinen Zimmerschlüssel verloren. [ikh **hah**buh **miy**nen **tsi**mmershlewsel fair**lo**ren]

Departure

I'm leaving/We're leaving tomorrow/today. — Ich reise/Wir reisen morgen/heute ab. [ikh **riy**zuh/veer **riy**zen **mor**gen/**hoy**tuh ap]

I'd like my bill, please. — Die Rechnung, bitte. [dee **rekh**noong **bit**tuh]

Would you call me a taxi, please. — Rufen Sie bitte ein Taxi. [**roo**fen zee **bit**tuh iyn **ta**xi]

It's been very nice here. — Es hat uns hier sehr gefallen. [es hat oons heer zair ge**fal**len]

Thank you very much. — Vielen Dank! [**fee**len dank]

Holiday cottage and holiday flat

We're looking for — **Wir suchen** [veer **zoo**khen]
- a holiday cottage — ein Ferienhaus [iyn **fair**yenhows]
- a holiday flat — eine Ferienwohnung [**iy**nuh **fair**yenvohnoong]
  - for 2/4 people — für 2/4 Personen [fewr tsviy/feer pair**soh**nen]
  - for 5 days/2 weeks. — für 5 Tage/2 Wochen. [fewr fewnf **tah**guh/tsviy **vo**khen]

How much is the flat/cottage? — Was kostet die Wohnung/das Haus? [vas **kos**tet dee **voh**noong/das hows]

How many rooms does the cottage have? — Wie viele Zimmer hat das Haus? [vee **feel**uh **tsi**mmer hat das hows]

Are there any additional costs? — Entstehen noch weitere Kosten? [ent**shtay**en nokk **viy**teruh **kos**ten]

How much is the deposit? — Wie hoch ist die Kaution? [vee hokh ist dee kowts**yon**]

Are pets/dogs allowed? — Sind Heimtiere/Hunde erlaubt? [zint **hiym**teeruh/**hoon**duh air**lowbt**]

HACKER~PSCHORR BRÄU
Altes
Hackerhaus
Sendlinger Gasse um 1570
Gasthaus
mit
Altmünchner Innenhof

Do we have to clean the flat/ cottage before we leave?
Müssen wir die Endreinigung übernehmen? [**mew**sen veer dee **end**riynigoong ewber**nay**men]

Where can I
make a phone call
do the laundry?

Wo kann man hier [voh kan man heer]
telefonieren [telefo**nee**ren]
Wäsche waschen? [**ve**shuh **va**shen]

Is there a supermarket around here?
Gibt es hier einen Supermarkt? [gibt es heer **iy**nen **zoo**permarkt]

Camping

Have you got room
for a tent
for a caravan
for a camper van?

Haben Sie Platz [**hah**ben zee plats]
für ein Zelt [fewr iyn tselt]
für einen Wohnwagen [fewr **iy**nen **vohn**vahgen]
für ein Wohnmobil? [fewr iyn **vohn**mobeel]

What's the charge
for one person
for a car
for a camper van
for a caravan
for a tent?

Was kostet der Platz [vas **ko**stet dair plats]
für eine Person [fewr **iy**nuh pair**sohn**]
für ein Auto [fewr iyn **ow**to]
für ein Wohnmobil [fewr iyn **vohn**mobeel]
für einen Wohnwagen [fewr **iy**nen **vohn**vahgen]
für ein Zelt? [fewr iyn tselt]

Do you also rent out
caravans
tents
bungalows?

Vermieten Sie auch [fair**mee**ten zee owkh]
Wohnwägen [**vohn**vaygen]
Zelte [**tsel**tuh]
Bungalows? [**boong**alows]

Where are the showers/ toilets?
Wo sind die Duschen/Toiletten? [voh zint dee **doo**shen/toi**let**ten]

Is there ... around here?
an electric hookup
a tap for filling up fresh water
a chemical toilet disposal point?

Gibt es hier [gibt es heer]
einen Stromanschluss [**iy**nen **shtrohm**anshloos]
einen Wasseranschluss [**iy**nen **va**sseranshloos]
eine Entleerungsmöglichkeit für das Chemieklo? [**iy**nuh ent**lair**oongsmerglikhkiyt fewr das ke**mee**klo]

When is the gate locked at night?
Wann wird nachts das Tor geschlossen? [van veert nakhts das tor ge**shlos**sen]

Is the campsite guarded at night?
Ist der Platz nachts bewacht? [ist dair plats nakhts be**vakht**]

Does the camping site have
a supermarket
a restaurant
public washing machines
cool boxes
a swimming pool
a playground?

Gibt es auf dem Campingplatz [gibt es owf dem campingplats]
einen Supermarkt [**iy**nen **zoo**permarkt]
ein Restaurant [iyn resto**rant**]
Münz-Waschmaschinen [**mewnts**vashmasheenen]
Kühlboxen [kewlboxen]
ein Schwimmbad [iyn **shvim**baht]
einen Spielplatz? [**iy**nen **shpeel**plats]

Youth hostel

Is there a youth hostel around here?	Gibt es hier eine Jugendherberge? [gibt es heer **iy**nuh **yoo**genthairbairguh]
How much is it per night	**Wie viel kostet eine Übernachtung** [vee**feel kos**tet **iy**nuh ewber**nakh**toong]
per person	pro Person [pro pair**sohn**]
with breakfast?	mit Frühstück? [mit **frew**shtewk]
We have a reservation.	Wir haben reserviert. [veer **hah**ben resair**veert**]
Do you have a family room?	Haben Sie ein Familienzimmer? [**hah**ben zee iyn fa**mee**lyentsimmer]

Accommodation

adapter	Adapter [a**da**pter]
air-conditioning	Klimaanlage [**klee**ma-anlaguh]
balcony	Balkon [bal**kohn**]
bathtub	Badewanne [**ba**duhvanuh]
bed	Bett [bet]
bed and breakfast	Privatzimmer [pri**vaht**-tsimmer]
bedlinen	Bettwäsche [**bet**veshuh]
blanket	Decke [**dek**kuh]
bill	Rechnung [**rekh**noong]
bottled gas	Gasflaschen *(Pl)* [**gas**flashen]
car park	Parkplatz [**park**plats]
chambermaid	Zimmermädchen [**tsi**mmermaydkhen]
clean *v.*	reinigen [**riy**nigen]
coffee machine	Kaffeemaschine [**ka**femasheenuh]
coins	Münzen [**mewn**tsen]
cot	Kinderbett [**kin**derbet]
cooker	Herd [haird]
cutlery	Besteck [be**shtek**]
crockery	Geschirr [ge**shir**]
dining room	Speisesaal [**shpiy**suhzahl]
drinking water	Trinkwasser [**trink**vasser]
electricity	Strom [shtrohm]
extra costs	Nebenkosten [**nay**benkosten]
family room	Familienzimmer [fa**mee**lyentsimmer]
fridge	Kühlschrank [**kewl**shrank]
garage	Garage [ga**rah**shuh]
guesthouse	Pension [pensyon]
heating	Heizung [**hiy**tsoong]
hire; borrow	leihen [**liy**en]
hire charge	Leihgebühr [**liy**gebewr]
holiday flat	Ferienwohnung [**fair**yen vohnoong]

I'm/We're staying for two days/weeks.	Ich bleibe/Wir bleiben 2 Tage/Wochen. [ikh **bliy**buh/veer **bliy**ben tsviy **tah**guh/**vo**khen]
I (don't) need bedlinen.	Ich brauche (keine)Bettwäsche. [ikh **brow**khuh (**kiy**nuh) **bet**weshuh]
When is the front door locked?	Wann wird die Eingangstür abgeschlossen? [van veert dee **iyn**gangstewr **ap**geshlossen]
How far is it to	**Wie weit ist es bis** [vee viyt ist es bis]
the beach	zum Strand [tsoom shtrand]
the town	zur Stadt [tsoor shtat]
the station?	zum Bahnhof? [tsoom **bahn**hof]
Is there a bus service to the centre of town?	Gibt es einen Bus ins Zentrum? [gibt es **iy**nen boos ins **tsen**troom]

key	Schlüssel [**shlew**sel]
kitchen	Küche [**kew**khuh]
lift	Aufzug [**owf**tsoog]
light	Licht [likht]
luggage	Gepäck [ge**pek**]
motorhome	Wohnmobil [**vohn**mobeel]
pillow	Kissen [**kis**sen]
plug	Stecker [**shtek**ker]
pots	Kochtöpfe [**kokh**terpfuh]
power point	Stromanschluss [**shtrohm**anshloos]
radio	Radio [**rahd**yo]
reduction	Ermäßigung [air**may**sigoong]
rent (out)	verleihen [fair**liy**en]
repair	reparieren [repa**ree**ren]
rubbish (bin)	Müll(eimer) [**mewl**(iymer)]
safe	Safe [**za**fe]
shower	Dusche [**doo**shuh]
sink	Spülbecken [**shpewl**bekken]
sleeping bag	Schlafsack [**shlaf**sak]
soap	Seife [**ziy**fuh]
socket	Steckdose [**shtek**dozuh]
tea towel	Geschirrtuch [ge**shir**tookh]
telephone	Telefon [tele**fon**]
tent peg	Hering [**hair**ing]
toilet	Toilette [toi**let**tuh]
toilet paper	Toilettenpapier [toi**let**tenpapeer]
towel	Handtuch [**hant**-tookh]
TV; television	Fernseher [**fairn**zayer]
wash	waschen [**va**shen]
washing machine	Waschmaschine [**va**shmasheenuh]
water (consumption)	Wasser(verbrauch) [**va**sser(fairbrowkh)]

Produce in abundance at Munich's Viktualienmarkt

Food and Drink

Is there ... around here?
a good/a reasonably cheap restaurant
a nice/a typical restaurant with regional/ international cuisine?

Wo gibt es hier [voh gibt es heer]
ein gutes/preiswertes Restaurant [iyn **goo**tes/**priy**svertes resto**rant**]
ein nettes Restaurant [iyn **net**tes resto**rant**] mit einheimischer/internationaler Küche? [mit **iyn**hiymisher/internatsyo**nah**ler **kew**khuh]

I'd like/We'd (just) like ..., please.
to have breakfast
to have lunch/dinner
a snack
something to drink.

Ich möchte/Wir möchten (nur) [ihk **mer**khtuh/veer **mer**khten (noor)]
frühstücken [**frew**shtewken]
zu Mittag-/Abendessen [tsoo **mit**tahg-/**ah**bentessen]
eine Kleinigkeit essen [**iy**nuh **kliy**nigkiyt **es**sen]
etwas trinken [**et**vas **trin**ken]

I'd like to reserve a table
for tonight/tomorrow night
at 7/8 o'clock
for 4/6 people.

Ich möchte einen Tisch bestellen [ikh **mer**khtuh **iy**nen tish be**stel**len]
für heute Abend/morgen Abend [fewr **hoy**tuh **ah**bent/**mor**gen **ah**bent]
um neunzehn Uhr/zwanzig Uhr [oom **noyn**tsayn oor/**tsvan**tsig oor]
für 4/6 Personen. [fewr feer/zex pair**soh**nen]

* Leider ist heute/morgen kein Tisch mehr frei. [**liy**der ist **hoy**tuh/**mor**gen kiyn tish mair friy]
I'm afraid we're fully booked for today/tomorrow.

* Wir haben morgen geschlossen. [veer **hah**ben **mor**gen ge**shlos**sen]
We're closed tomorrow.

ve reserved a table. The ame is ... — Ich habe einen Tisch bestellt auf den Namen ... [ikh **hah**buh **iy**nen tish bes**telt** owf den **nah**men]

. table for 2/4, please. — Einen Tisch für 2/4 Personen, bitte. [**iy**nen tish fewr tsviy/feer pair**soh**nen **bit**tuh]

ſay we sit at this table? — Ist dieser Tisch frei? [ist **dee**zer tish friy]
; this seat taken? — Ist dieser Platz besetzt? [ist **dee**zer plats be**zetst**]

o you have a high chair? — Haben Sie einen Kinderstuhl? [**hah**ben zee **iy**nen **kin**dershtool]

xcuse me, where's the toilet? — Wo ist die Toilette, bitte? [voh ist dee toi**let**tuh **bit**tuh]

low to order

xcuse me, please. — Herr Ober/Bedienung! [hair **oh**ber/be**dee**noong]

ould I have the menu/wine st, please. — Die Speisekarte/Getränkekarte, bitte! [dee **shpiy**suhkartuh/ge**tren**kuhkartuh **bit**tuh]
/hat can you recommend? — Was empfehlen Sie? [vas em**pfay**len zee]

l have — **Ich möchte/Ich nehme** [ikh **mer**khtuh/ ikh **nay**muh]
- (no) soup — (keine) eine Suppe [(**kiy**nuh) **zoo**puh]
- the dish of the day — das Tagesgericht [das **tah**gesgerikht]
- menu number 1/2 — Menü Nummer 1/2 [me**new noo**mer iyns/tsviy]
- this — dies [dees]
  - as a starter/as the main course/for dessert. — als Vorspeise/Hauptspeise/Nachspeise. [als **for**shpiysuh/**howpt**shpiysuh/**nahkh**shpiysuh]

o you have any regional pecialities? — Was ist typisch für diese Region? [vas ist **tew**pish fewr **dee**zuh reg**yon**]
ould I have pasta/rice ıstead of chips, please? — Ich möchte bitte Nudeln/Reis statt Pommes frites. [ikh **merkh**tuh **bit**tuh **noo**deln/riys statt pom **frit**]

or him/her/ ıe children ..., please. — **Für das Kind/die Kinder bitte** [fewr das kind/dee **kin**der **bit**tuh]
- a half portion/half portions — einen Kinderteller/Kinderteller [**iy**nen **kin**derteller/**kin**derteller]

German sausages

Many German sausages and hams have achieved worldwide fame, notably Frankfurter sausages and Westphalian ham, but there numerous regional varieties.

There are said to be some 1,500 varieties of sausages or **Würste [vewrstuh]**. A **Wurst** is not necessarily the same as the British *banger*, although some such as **Bratwürste** are fried or grilled. A few varieties are boiled, such as the **Knackwurst**, **Bockwurst** and **Frankfurter**. Many others such as **Bierwurst** (goes well with beer) or **Fleischwurst** are sliced thinly or spread (**Leberwurst**) and eaten with bread. Preserved sausages, **Rohwürste**, are made from lean pork, bacon and beef and then smoked or air-dried. The best-known are **Kochsalami**, **Pfeffersalami** and **Cervelatwurst**.

Do you have a vegetarian dish?	Gibt es ein vegetarisches Gericht? [gibt es iyn vege**tar**ishes ge**rikht**]
Is this dish (very) hot/sweet/ rich?	Ist dieses Gericht (sehr) scharf/süß/fett? [ist **dee**zes ge**rikht** (zair) sharf/z-ews/fet]
To drink, I'd like/we'd like	**Zu trinken möchte ich/möchten wir bitte** [tsoo **trin**ken **mer**khtuh ikh/**mer**khten veer **bit**tuh
a glass	ein Glas [iyn glas]
a (half) bottle	eine (halbe) Flasche [**iy**nuh (**hal**buh) **fla**shuh]
(half) a litre of red/white wine.	einen (halben) Liter Rot-/Weißwein. [**iy**nen (**hal**ben) **lee**ter **roht**-/**viys**viyn]
Do you sell wine by the glass, too?	Haben Sie auch offenen Wein? [**hah**ben zee owkh **o**ffenen viyn]
Thank you, that's all.	Danke, das ist alles. [**dan**kuh das ist **a**lles]
Could I have . . ., please?	**Kann ich noch . . ., haben?** [kan ikh nokh **hah**ben
some more bread/gravy	etwas Brot/Soße [**et**vas brot/**zo**suh]
another beer	ein Bier [iyn beer]
Cheers!/Your health!	Prost!/Auf Ihr Wohl! [prost/owf eer vohl]
Do you mind if I smoke?	Stört es Sie, wenn ich rauche? [shtert es zee ven ikh **row**khuh]

Complaints

That's not what I ordered!	Das habe ich nicht bestellt! [das **hah**buh ikh nikht be**shtelt**]
Have you forgotten my food/ my drink?	Haben Sie mein Essen/mein Getränk vergessen [**hah**ben zee miyn **e**ssen/miyn ge**trenk** fair**ge**ssen]
I'm sorry but	**Es tut mir leid, aber** [es toot meer liyd **a**ber]
the soup/the food is cold	die Suppe/das Essen ist kalt [dee **zoo**puh/das **e**ssen ist kalt]
the meat is tough/not cooked through.	das Fleisch ist zäh/nicht durch. [das fliysh ist tsay/nikht durkh]
There seems to be a mistake in the bill	Ich glaube, die Rechnung stimmmt nicht. [ikh **glow**buh dee **rekh**noong shtimt nikht]
What is this, please?	Was ist das? [vas ist das]
I didn't have that!	Das habe ich nicht bestellt. [das **hah**buh ikh nikht be**shtelt**]

Wine notes

If Liebfraumilch is the extent to which you've sampled German wines, then you'll be in for a pleasant surprise.

First, the Liebfraumilch on offer in Germany is far superior to the exported bottles. Second, there are many more German wines to sample: from honeyed sweet or rich dry Riesling, to fruity Müller-Thurgau to the spicier, fuller Gewürztraminer.

Although Germany majors on whites, French reds are readily available. Some indigenous reds (such as those produced in Baden) are very palatable.

Beer and schnaps

In Germany **Bier** [beer] *(beer)* is the national drink. But unlike Britain, there are almost no "national" brands of beer. Instead each region has its own particular breweries, and beer drinkers (nine out of ten German adults) tend to stick very much with the same brand. Low-alcohol and non-alcoholic beers are also popular in Germany. They are brewed in the traditional manner so they retain their full flavour.

Schnaps [shnaps] is a collective term for all strong drinks. **Korn** is a colourless spirit made from grain, i.e. wheat, oats or barley. It has either a neutral taste or can be flavoured with juniper or caraway. **Weinbrand** [**viyn**brant], the German equivalent of cognac, is a high quality brandy distilled from grapes, while **Obstweinbrand** [**opst**viynbrant] is a brandy made from fully fermented fruit such as cherries, plums, apricots, peaches or blackberries. The best known of these is the cherry **Kirsch** [kirsh].

A glass of schnaps is usually drunk chilled and neat as an accompaniment to beer or after a rich meal to help digestion.

Could we have ..., please?	**Es fehlt noch/Bringen Sie uns bitte noch** [es faylt nokh/**bri**ngen zee oons **bit**tuh nokh]
some bread	Brot [broht]
some cutlery	Besteck [be**shtek**]
another knife	ein Messer [iyn **mes**ser]
another fork	eine Gabel [**iy**nuh **gah**bel]
another (tea) spoon	einen (kleinen) Löffel [**iy**nen (**kliy**nen) **ler**fel]
another plate	einen Teller [**iy**nen **tel**ler]
another glass	ein Glas [iyn glahs]
oil and vinegar	Essig und Öl [**es**sig oont erl]
salt and pepper	Salz und Pfeffer [salts oont **pfef**fer]
an ashtray	einen Aschenbecher [**iy**nen **a**shenbekher]
napkins	Servietten [**zair**vyetten]
toothpicks	Zahnstocher. [**tsahn**shtokher]

Paying the bill

Could I have the bill, please.	Zahlen/Die Rechnung, bitte! [**tsah**len/dee **rekh**noong **bit**tuh]
All together, please.	(Ich zahle) alles zusammen. [ikh **tsah**luh **al**les tsoo**zam**men]
Separate bills, please.	Wir zahlen getrennt. [veer **tsah**len ge**trent**]
Could I have a receipt?	Ich möchte eine Quittung, bitte. [ikh **merkh**tuh **iy**nuh **kwi**toong **bit**tuh]
Hat es geschmeckt? [hat es ge**shmekt**]	Did you enjoy it?
Waren Sie zufrieden? [varen zee **tsoo**freeden]	Was everything O.K.?
It was very good, thank you.	Danke, es war sehr gut. [**dan**kuh es var zair goot]
That's for you.	Das ist für Sie. [das ist fewr zee]
Keep the change.	Stimmt so! [shtimt zo]

Food

Fruhstück [**frew**shtewk]	**Breakfast**
Brot [broht]	bread
Brötchen [**brert**khen]	roll
Butter [b**oo**ter]	butter
Frühstücksflocken [frewshtewks**flok**ken]	cereal
Frühstücksspeck [frewshtewks-**shpek**]	bacon
Honig [**hoh**nig]	honey
Joghurt [**yoh**goort]	yogurt
Käse [**kay**suh]	cheese
Kaffee [**kaf**fay]	coffee
schwarz [shvarts]	black
koffeinfrei [koffuh**een**friy]	decaffeinated
mit/ohne Milch [mit/**oh**nuh milkh]	with/without milk
mit Zucker/Süßstoff [mit **tsoo**ker/**zews**-shtof]	with sugar/sweetener
Kakao [kak**kow**]	cocoa
Kräutertee [kroyter**tay**]	herbal tea
Marmelade [marme**lah**duh]	jam
Milch [milkh]	milk
warm/kalt [varm/kalt]	hot/cold
Orangensaft [**oran**shenzaft]	orange juice
Rührei [**rew**riy]	scrambled egg
Schinken [**shin**ken]	ham
Spiegelei [**shpee**geliy]	fried egg
Tee (mit Zitrone) [tay (mit tsit**roh**nuh]	tea (with lemon)
Toast [toast]	toast
Vollkornbrot [follkorn**broht**]	wholemeal bread
weich gekochtes Ei [**viykh**gekokhtes iy]	soft-boiled egg
Wurst [voorst]	sausage

Kleine Mahlzeiten [**kliy**nuh **mahl**tsiyten]	**Snacks**
belegtes Brot [be**layg**tes brot]	sandwich
mit Käse [mit **kay**suh]	cheese
mit Wurst [mit voorst]	cold meat
mit Schinken [mit **shin**ken]	ham
Bockwurst [**bok**voorst]	Frankfurter
Bratwurst [**brat**voorst]	fried sausage
Brezel [**bray**tsel]	pretzel
Fischsemmel [**fish**semmel]	roll with pickled herring
Kalte Platte [**kal**tuh **plat**tuh]	platter with cold meat, cheese and bread
Käseplatte [**kay**suhplattuh]	ploughman's lunch
Omelette [om**let**]	omelette
Pommes frites [pom **frit**]	chips
mit Ketschup/Majonäse [mit **ket**chup/miyo**nay**zuh]	with ketchup/mayonnaise
Strammer Max [**stram**mer max]	fried egg served on smoked ham and bread
Wurstsemmel [**voorst**semmel]	roll with cold meat

Vorspeisen [**for**shpiysen]	**Starters**
gemischte Vorspeisen [ge**mish**tuh **for**shpiysen]	mixed starters
Knoblauchbrot [**knob**lowkhbroht]	garlic bread
Krabbencocktail [**krab**bencocktail]	prawn cocktail
Pastete [pa**stay**tuh]	pâté
Räucherlachs [**roy**kherlax]	smoked salmon
Salat [sa**laht**]	salad
gemischter Salat [ge**mish**ter sa**laht**]	mixed salad
Tomatensalat [to**mah**tensalaht]	tomato salad
Gurkensalat [**goor**kensalaht]	cucumber salad
Meeresfrüchtesalat [**mair**esfrewkhtuhsalaht]	seafood salad
mit Essig und Öl [mit **e**sig oont erl]	with French dressing
Weinbergschnecken [**viyn**bergshnekken]	snails

Suppen [**z**oopen]	**Soups**
Bouilion (mit Ei) [**bool**yon (mit iy)]	clear soup (with egg)
Gemüsesuppe [ge**mew**suhzoopuh]	vegetable soup
Gulaschsuppe [**gool**ashzoopuh]	thick, stew-like soup
Hühnersuppe [**hew**nerzoopuh]	chicken soup
Leberknödelsuppe [**lay**berknerdelzoopuh]	clear soup with dumplings made of liver
Ochsenschwanzsuppe [**o**khsenshvantszoopuh]	oxtail soup
Pfannkuchensuppe [**pfan**kookhenzoopuh]	clear soup with strips of pancakes

Fische und Meeresfrüchte [**fi**shuh oont **mair**esfrewkhtuh]	**Fish and seafood**
Aal [ahl]	eel
Austern [**ow**stern]	oysters
Fisch [fish]	fish
gebacken/gekocht/geräuchert [ge**bak**ken/ge**kokht**/ge**roy**khert]	baked/boiled/ smoked
frittiert/gebacken/gegrillt [frit**teert**/ge**bak**ken/ge**grilt**]	deep-fried/fried/grilled
Forelle [fo**rel**luh]	trout
Hummer [**hoo**mer]	lobster
Kabeljau [kahbel**yow**]	cod
Krebs [krebs]	crab
Lachs [lax]	salmon
Languste [lan**goo**stuh]	crayfish
Makrele [mak**ray**luh]	mackerel
Miesmuscheln [**mees**moosheln]	mussles
Riesengarnelen [**ree**zengarnellen]	king prawns
Sardellen [zar**del**len]	anchovies
Schellfisch [**shell**fish]	haddock
Scholle [**shol**luh]	plaice
Seezunge [**say**tsoonguh]	sole
Tintenfisch [**tin**tenfish]	squid
Venusmuscheln [**vee**noosmoosheln]	clams

Fleisch(gerichte) [fliysh(ge**rikh**tuh)]	**Meat dishes**
Eintopf [**iyn**topf]	stew/casserole
Eisbein [**iys**biyn]	knuckle of pork
Filet [fil**lay**]	fillet
Fleischklößchen [**fliysh**klerskhen]	meatballs
Grillteller [**gril**teller]	mixed grill
Gulasch [**goo**lash]	stew
Hackfleisch [**hak**fliysh]	minced meat
Hammelfleisch [**ham**melfliysh]	mutton
Kalbfleisch [**kalb**fliysh]	veal
Kotelett [kot**let**]	chop
Lammfleisch [**lam**fliysh]	lamb
Leber [**lay**ber]	liver
Ragout [ra**goo**]	casserole
Rindfleisch [**rind**fliysh]	beef
Rinderbraten [**rin**derbrahten]	roast beef
Rinderlende [**rin**derlenduh]	sirloin
Rindsroulade [**rinds**roolahduh]	slices of rolled-up beef stuffed with bacon
Sauerbraten [**zow**erbrahten]	roast beef in vinegar and red-wine sauce
saure Lunge mit Semmelknödeln [**zow**ruh **loo**nguh mit **sem**melknerdeln]	lung casserole, served with bread dumplings
Schnitzel [**shnit**sel]	escalope
Schweinefleisch [**shviy**nuhfliysh]	pork
Steak [steak]	steak
englisch/medium/durchgebraten [**eng**lish/**me**dium/**doorkh**gebrahten]	medium-rare/medium well-done

Geflügel/Wild [ge**flew**gel/veeld]	**Poultry/Game**
Brathähnchen [**brat**haynkhen]	roast chicken
Ente [**en**tuh]	duck
Gans [gans]	goose
Huhn/Hähnchen [hoon/**hayn**khen]	chicken
Kaninchen [kan**neen**khen]	rabbit
Rebhuhn [**rayb**hoon]	partridge
Rehbraten [**ray**brahten]	venison
Truthahn [**troot**hahn]	turkey
Wildschweinbraten [**veelt**shviynbrahten]	roast wild boar

Beilagen [**biy**lagen]	**Side dishes**
Bratkartoffeln [**braht**kartoffeln]	roast potatoes
Kartoffeln [kar**toff**eln]	potatoes
Kartoffelknödel [kar**toff**elknerdel]	potato dumplings
Kartoffelpüree [kar**toff**elpewray]	mashed potatoes
Nudeln [**noo**deln]	noodles/pasta
Reis [riys]	rice
Semmelknödel [**sem**melknerdel]	bread dumplings
Spätzle [**shpets**luh]	Swabian type of noodles

Salate und Gemüse [za**lah**tuh oont ge**mew**suh]	**Salads and vegetables**
Blaukraut [**blow**krowt]	red cabbage
Blumenkohl [**bloo**menkohl]	cauliflower
Fenchel [**fen**khel]	fennel
Linsen [**lin**zen]	lentils
Maiskolben [**miys**kolben]	corn-on-the-cob
Pilze [**pil**tsuh]	mushrooms
Rosenkohl [**ro**zenkohl]	Brussels sprouts
Rote Bete [**roh**tuh **bay**tuh]	beetroot
Sauerkraut [**zow**erkrowt]	pickled cabbage
Spargel [**shpar**gel]	asparagus
Stangensellerie [**shta**ngenzeleree]	celery

▶ **(Fruit and vegetables, see page 62)**

Käse [**kay**suh]	**Cheese**
Blauschimmelkäse [**blow**shimmelkaysuh]	blue cheese
geriebener Käse [ge**ree**bener **kay**suh]	grated cheese
Hüttenkäse [**hew**tenkaysuh]	cottage cheese
Harzerkäse [**har**tserkaysuh]	aromatic cheese from the Harz area
Münsterkäse [**mewn**sterkaysuh]	mild to aromatic cow's milk cheese
Quark [kwark]	curd cheese
Räucherkäse [**roy**kherkaysuh]	smoked cheese
Tilsiter [**til**siter]	firm cow's milk cheese
Ziegenkäse [**tsee**genkaysuh]	goat's cheese

Süßspeisen [**zews**-shpiyzen]	**Desserts**
Apfelkuchen [**a**pfelkookhen]	apple tart
Bienenstich [**bee**nenshtikh]	yeast cake filled with cream and topped with almonds
Brotauflauf [**broht**owflowf]	bread and butter pudding
Gebäck [ge**bek**]	pastry/biscuits
Hefezopf [**hay**fuhtsopf]	cake made of yeast dough
Käsekuchen [**kay**suhkookhen]	cheesecake
Kaiserschmarren [**kiy**zershmarn]	sweet pancakes torn in bits
Kuchen [**koo**khen]	cake
Milchreis [**milkh**riys]	rice pudding
Obstsalat [**opst**salaht]	fruit salad
Pudding [**poo**ding]	blancmange
Sahnetorte [**zah**nuhtortuh]	gâteau
Schlagsahne [**shlag**zahnuh]	whipped cream
Schokoladenpudding [shoko**lah**den **poo**ding]	chocolate blancmange
Schwarzwälder Kirschtorte [shvarts**vel**der **kirsh**tortuh]	Black Forest gâteau
Stollen [**shtol**len]	Christmas speciality
Streuselkuchen [**stroy**zelkookhen]	crumble cake
Vanillesauce [va**nil**luhzozuh]	custard

Eis [iys]	**Ice-cream**
Eiskaffee [**iys**kafe]	iced coffee
Erdbeer [**aird**bair]	strawberry
Früchtebecher [**frewkh**tuhbekher]	fruit sundae
gemischtes Eis [ge**mish**tes iys]	mixed ice-cream
mit Sahne [mit **zah**nuh]	with cream
Haselnuss [**hah**zelnoos]	hazelnut
Himbeer [**him**bair]	raspberry
Schokolade [shoko**lah**duh]	chocolate
Vanille [va**nil**luh]	vanilla
Zitrone [tsi**troh**nuh]	lemon

Drinks

Alkoholische Getränke [alko**hoh**lishuh ge**tren**kuh]	**Alcoholic drinks**
Aperitif [aperi**teef**]	apéritif
Apfelwein [apfel**viyn**]	cider
Bier [beer]	beer
alkoholfreies [alko**hohl**friyes]	alcohol-free
Flaschenbier [**fla**shenbeer]	bottled beer
vom Faß [fom fas]	draught
helles Bier [**hel**les beer]	lager
dunkles Bier [**doonk**les beer]	ale
Champagner/Sekt [sham**pan**yuh/zekt]	champagne/sparkling wine
Grog [grog]	toddy
Kognak [**kon**yak]	brandy
Likör [lik**ker**]	liqueur
Wein [viyn]	wine
trocken/halbtrocken [**trok**ken/**halb**trokken]	dry/medium dry
lieblich/süß [**leeb**likh/zews]	sweet
weiß/rot/rosé [viys/roht/roh**zay**]	white/red/rosé
Whisky [**vis**ky]	whisky
- Soda/mit Eis [**zo**da/mit iys]	soda/on the rocks

Erfrischungsgetränke [air**fri**shoongsgetrenkuh]	**Soft drinks**
Apfelsaft [**a**pfelzaft]	apple juice
Cola [**koh**luh]	Coke
Fruchtsaft [**frookht**zaft]	fruit juice
Limonade [limmo**nah**duh]	fizzy drink
Milch [milkh]	milk
Mineralwasser [mine**ral**vasser]	mineral water
mit/ohne Kohlensäure [mit/**oh**nuh **koh**lenzoyruh]	sparkling/still
Orangensaft [o**ran**shenzaft]	orange juice
frisch gepresst– [frish gepresst]	freshly squeezed
Tonic [**to**nic]	tonic water

▶ **(Hot drinks, see breakfast, page 44)**

The 'Goldener Reiter', one of the symbols of Dresden

Sightseeing

Tourist information

Is there a tourist information office in the area? — Gibt es hier ein Fremdenverkehrsamt? [gibt es heer iyn **frem**denfairkairsamt]

Are there — **Gibt es** [gibt es]
guided tours — Führungen [**few**roongen]
sightseeing tours of the city? — Stadtrundfahrten? [**shtat**roondfahrten]

Do you have — **Haben Sie** [**hah**ben zee]
a street map — einen Stadtplan [**iy**nen **shtat**plahn]
a map of the city centre — eine Karte der Innenstadt [**iy**nuh **kar**tuh dair **in**nenshtat]
a map of the area — eine Karte der Umgebung [**iy**nuh **kar**tuh dair oom**gay**boong]
a map of the underground — einen U-Bahn-Plan [**iy**nen **oo**bahnplahn]
brochures — Prospektmaterial [pro**spekt**matairyal]
a list of hotels — ein Hotelverzeichnis [iyn ho**tel**fairtsiykhnis]
a list of restaurants — ein Restaurantverzeichnis [iyn resto**rant**fairtsiykhnis]
a programme of events — einen Veranstaltungskalender [**iy**nen fair**an**shtaltoongskal**en**der]
for this week/for the festival? — für diese Woche/für die Festwoche? [fewr **dee**zuh **vo**khuh/fewr dee **fest**vokhuh]

Could you book a room for me? — Können Sie mir ein Zimmer reservieren? [**ker**nen zee meer iyn **tsi**mmer resair**vee**ren]

What are the places of interest around here? — Welche Sehenswürdigkeiten gibt es hier? [**vel**khuh **zay**ensvewrdigkiyten gibt es heer]

Sightseeing

abbey	Abtei [**ap**tiy]
altar	Altar [al**tahr**]
ancient; antique	antik [an**teek**]
architecture	Architektur [arkhitek**toor**]
art	Kunst [koonst]
artist	Künstler [**kewnst**ler]
arts and crafts	Kunstgewerbe [koonstgevairbuh]
Baroque	Barock [ba**rokk**]
basilica	Basilika [ba**zi**lika]
botanical gardens	botanischer Garten [bo**tah**nisher **gar**ten]
bridge	Brücke [**brew**kuh]
building	Gebäude [ge**boy**duh]
castle	Burg [boorg]; Schloss [shloss]
cathedral	Kathedrale [katay**drah**luh]
cave	Höhle [**her**luh]
ceiling fresco	Deckenmalerei [**dek**kenmahlairiy]
cemetery	Friedhof [**freed**hof]
century	Jahrhundert [yar**hoon**dert]
ceramics	Keramik [ke**rah**mik]
chapel	Kapelle [ka**pel**luh]
Christian	christlich [**krist**likh]
church	Kirche [**keer**khuh]
convent	Kloster [**kloh**ster]
copy	Kopie [ko**pee**]
courtyard	Hof [hohf]
cross	Kreuz [kroyts]
crown	Krone [**kroh**nuh]
drawing	Zeichnung [**tsiy**khnoong]
emperor	Kaiser [**kiy**zer]
empress	Kaiserin [**kiy**zerin]
epoch	Epoche [e**pok**khuh]
excavation	Ausgrabung [**ows**grahboong]
exhibit	Exponat [expo**naht**]
façade	Fassade [fa**zah**duh]
forest	Wald [valt]
fortress	Festung [**fes**toong]
gallery	Galerie [galle**ree**]
garden	Garten [**gar**ten]
glass	Glas [glahs]
gorge	Schlucht [shlookht]
Gothic	gotisch [**goh**tish]
grave	Grab [grahb]
grotto	Grotte [**grot**tuh]
harbour	Hafen [**hah**fen]
history	Geschichte [ge**shikh**tuh]

inscription	Inschrift [**in**shrift]
island	Insel [**in**zel]
king	König [**ker**nig]
lake	See [zay]
landscape	Landschaft [**lant**shaft]
library	Bibliothek [biblio**tayk**]
market	Markt [markt]
medieval	mittelalterlich [**mit**telalterlikh]
memorial	Gedenkstätte [ge**denk**stettuh]
monastery	Kloster [**kloh**ster]
monument	Denkmal [**denk**mahl]
mountain	Berg [bairg]
nature reserve	Naturschutzgebiet [na**toor**shootsgebeet]
old town	Altstadt [**alt**shtat]
painting	Gemälde [ge**mel**duh]
panorama	Rundblick [**roond**blik]
park	Park [park]
pedestrian precinct	Fußgängerzone [**foos**gengertsohnuh]
picture	Bild [bilt]
port	Hafen [**hah**fen]
prehistoric	prähistorisch [**pray**histohrish]
queen	Königin [**ker**nigin]
ramparts	Stadtmauer [**shtat**mower]
relief	Relief [re**lyef**]
religion	Religion [relig**yon**]
remains	Überreste [**ew**ber-restuh]
Renaissance	Renaissance [renay**sonce**]
restore	rastaurieren [restow**ree**ren]
Romanesque	romanisch [ro**mah**nish]
roof	Dach [dakh]
ruin(s)	Ruine [roo**ee**nuh]
square	Platz [plats]
statue	Statue [**shta**too-uh]
style	Stil [shteel]
synagogue	Synagoge [zoona**goh**guh]
temple	Tempel [**tem**pel]
theatre	Theater [tay**ah**ter]
tomb	Grabmal [**grahb**mal]
tourist guide	Fremdenführer [**frem**denfewrer]
tower	Turm [toorm]
town hall	Rathaus [**raht**hows]
traditions	Brauchtum [**browkh**toom]
valley	Tal [tahl]
view	Aussicht [**ows**zikht]
waterfalll	Wasserfall [**va**sserfahl]

Visiting the sights

I'd like/We'd like to visit	**Ich möchte/Wir möchten ... besichtigen.** [ikh **mer**khtuh/veer **mer**khten be**zikh**tigen]
the cathedral/church	die Kathedrale/Kirche [dee katay**drah**luh/**keer**khuh]
the palace	den Palast [dayn pa**last**]
the castle.	das Schloss [das shloss]
What are the opening hours of the exhibition/the museum?	Wann ist die Ausstellung/das Museum geöffnet? [van ist dee **ows**-shteloong/das moo**zay**-oom ge-**er**fnet]
Is there a guided tour in English?	Gibt es eine englische Führung? [gibt es **iy**nuh **eng**lishuh **few**roong]
When does it start?	Wann beginnt sie? [van be**gint** zee]
How much is it?	Was kostet sie? [vas **kos**tet zee]
How long does it take?	Wie lange dauert sie? [vee **la**nguh **dow**ert zee]
1/2 ticket(s) for adults/children, please.	Bitte eine Karte/zwei Karten für Erwachsene/Kinder. [**bit**tuh **iy**nuh **kar**tuh/tsviy **kar**ten fewr air**vakh**senuh/**kin**der]
Are there special rates for children/students/senior citizens?	Gibt es Ermäßigung für Kinder/Studenten/ Senioren? [gibt es air**may**sigoong fewr **kin**der/shtoo**den**ten/sen**yor**en]
* Wegen Renovierung geschlossen. [**vay**gen reno**veer**oong ge**shlos**sen]	Closed for renovation.
Can I use my video camera?	Darf ich hier filmen? [darf ikh heer **fil**men]
Do you have a guide in English?	Haben Sie einen Führer in englischer Sprache? [**hah**ben zee **iy**nen **few**rer in **eng**lisher **shprah**khuh]

Excursions

How much is the excursion to ...?	Wie viel kostet die Fahrt nach ...? [vee feel **kos**tet dee fahrt nahkh]
Do we have to pay for the meal/admission charges?	Ist das Essen/Sind die Eintrittspreise extra zu bezahlen? [ist das **es**sen/zint dee **iyn**tritspriysuh **ex**tra tsoo be**tsah**len]
2 tickets for today's excursion/tomorrow's excursion/for the excursion at 10 o'clock, please.	Bitte zwei Plätze für den Ausflug heute/morgen/um 10 Uhr. [**bit**tuh tsviy **plet**suh fewr den **ows**floog **hoy**tuh/**mor**gen/oom tsayn oor]
When/Where do we meet?	Wann/Wo ist der Treffpunkt? [van/voh ist dair **treff**poonkt]
When do we get back?	Wann kommen wir zurück? [van **kom**men veer tsoo**rewk**]
Do we have	**Haben wir** [**hah**ben veer]
any free time	freie Zeit zur Verfügung [**friy**uh tsiyt tsoor fair**few**goong]
time to go shopping?	Zeit für Einkäufe? [tsiyt fewr **iyn**koyfuh]

Hang-gliding is a popular pursuit in the uplands of the Bavarian Forest as well as in the Alps

Active Pursuits

At the beach and at the swimming pool

Is there ... around here?	**Gibt es hier** [gibt es heer]
an open-air/indoor swimming pool	ein Freibad/Hallenbad [iyn **friy**baht/**hal**lenbaht]
a place to hire boats?	einen Bootsverleih? [**iy**nen **bohts**fairliy]
How far is it to the beach?	Wie weit ist es bis zum Strand? [vee viyt ist es bis tsoom shtrand]
When is low tide/high tide?	Wann ist Ebbe/Flut? [van ist **eb**buh/floot]
Is there a strong current?	Ist die Strömung gefährlich? [ist dee **shtrer**moong ge**fair**likh]
Is it dangerous for children?	Ist es für Kinder gefährlich? [ist es fewr **kin**der ge**fair**likh]
Are there jellyfish in the water?	Gibt es Quallen im Wasser? [gibt es **kwal**len im **va**sser]
I'd like/We'd like to hire	**Ich möchte/Wir möchten ... mieten.** [ikh **merkh**tuh/veer **merkh**ten **mee**ten]
a pedal/rowing/sailing boat/motorboat	ein Tret-/Ruder-/Segelboot/Motorboot [iyn **tret**-/**roo**der-/**zay**gelboht/mo**tor**boht]
a deckchair	einen Liegestuhl [**iy**nen **lee**guhshtool]
a surfboard	ein Surfbrett [iyn **zurf**brett]
a pair of water skis.	Wasserski [**va**ssershee]
How much is it	**Was kostet das** [vas **kos**tet das]
per (half) hour	pro (halbe) Stunde [pro (**hal**buh) **shtoon**duh]
per week?	pro Woche? [pro **vo**khuh]
I'd like a coaching session.	Ich möchte eine Trainerstunde. [ikh **merkh**tuh **iy**nuh **tray**nershtoonduh]

Danger signs

Gefährlich	dangerous
Baden/Springen verboten!	no swimming/jumping
Sturmwarnung	storm warning
Nur für Schwimmer!	swimmers only

I'd like to take	**Ich möchte einen ... machen.** [ikh **mer**khtuh **iy**nen **ma**khen]
sailing lessons	Segelkurs [**zay**gelkoors]
surfing lessons	Surfkurs [**zurf**koors]
diving lessons.	Tauchkurs [**towkh**koors]
I'm a beginner.	Ich bin Anfänger. [ikh bin **an**fenger]
I'm an experienced surfer.	Ich bin ein fortgeschrittener Surfer. [ikh bin iyn **fort**geshrittener **zurf**er]

Sports

Is there ... around here?	**Gibt es hier** [gibt es heer]
a place to hire bikes	Fahrräder zu mieten [**fahr**ayder tsoo **mee**ten]
a (crazy) golf course	einen (Mini)Golfplatz [**iy**nen (**mi**ni)**golf**plats]
a tennis court	einen Tennisplatz? [**iy**nen **ten**nisplats]
Where can I	**Wo kann man hier** [voh kan man heer]
go canoeing	Kajak fahren [**ki**yak **fah**ren]
go bowling/horse-riding	kegeln/reiten [**kay**geln/**riy**ten]
play squash/table tennis/tennis?	Squash/Tischtennis/Tennis spielen? [squash/**tish**tennis/tenis s**hpee**len]
Where can I take	**Wo kann ich hier einen ... belegen?** [voh kan ikh heer **iy**nen belegen]
riding lessons	Reitkurs [**riyt**koors]
tennis lessons?	Tenniskurs [**ten**niskoors]
Is swimming/fishing allowed here?	Darf man hier baden/angeln? [darf man heer **bah**den/**ang**eln]
Do you play chess?	Spielen Sie Schach? [**shpee**len zee shakh]
Do you mind if I join in?	Kann ich mitspielen? [kan ikh **mit**shpeelen]
I'd like/We'd like to see	**Ich möchte/Wir möchten ... sehen.** [ikh **merkh**tuh/veer **merkh**ten **zay**en]
the tennis/football match	das Tennis-/Fußballspiel [das **ten**nis-/**foos**balshpeel]
the competition	den Wettkampf [den **vet**kampf]
the race	das Rennen [das **ren**nen]
the cycle race	das Radrennen [das **rahd**rennen]
the horse-race.	das Pferderennen [das **pfair**duhrennen]
When does the event start?	Wann beginnt die Veranstaltung? [van be**gint** dee fair**an**shtaltoong]
Where does it take place?	Wo findet sie statt? [voh **fin**det zee shtat]

Nature, environment, adventure

We'd like	**Wir möchten** [veer **merkh**ten]
to go on a bicycle tour	eine Radtour machen [**iy**nuh **rahd**toor makhen]
to go hiking	eine Bergtour machen [**iy**nuh **bairg**toor makhen]
to go trekking	wandern [**van**dern]
in the nature reserve.	im Naturschutzgebiet [im na**toor**shootsgebeet]
in the national park.	im Nationalpark. [im natsyo**nal**park]

Active pursuits

aerobics	Aerobic [ae**ro**bic]
arm bands	Schwimmflügel [**shvim**flewgel]
badminton	Federball [**fay**derbal]
ball	Ball [bal]
basketball	Basketball [**bahs**ketbal]
bay	Bucht [bookht]
billiards	Billiard [**bil**yard]
changing rooms	Umkleidekabinen [**oom**kliyduhkabeenen]
diving equipment	Taucherausrüstung [**tow**kherowsrewstoong]
flippers	Schwimmflossen [**shvim**flossen]
gymnastics	Gymnastik [goom**nas**tik]
health club	Fitnesscenter [**fit**nesscenter]
horse	Pferd [pfaird]
jogging	Jogging [**jog**ging]
playground	Spielplatz [**shpeel**plats]
pony	Pony [pony]
ride	Ausritt [**ows**ritt]
rubber dinghy	Schlauchboot [**shlowkh**boht]
sauna	Sauna [**zow**na]
shade	Schatten [**shat**ten]
shells	Muscheln [**moo**sheln]
skate	Schlittschuh laufen [**shlit**shoo **low**fen]
ski	Ski [shee] *n.*; Ski fahren [**shee fah**ren] *v.*
sled	Schlitten [**shlit**ten]
snorkel	Schnorchel [**shnor**khel]
snow	Schnee [shnay]
solarium	Solarium [so**lar**yoom]
stadium	Stadion [**shta**dyon]
storm	Sturm [stoorm]
suntan lotion	Sonnenmilch [**zon**nenmilkh]
volleyball	Volleyball [**vol**leebal]
wave	Welle [**vel**luh]

Do you have	**Haben Sie** [**hah**ben zee]
a hiking map	eine Wanderkarte [**iy**nuh **van**derkartuh]
a map of cycle paths	eine Radwanderkarte [**iy**nuh **rahd**vanderkartuh]
any suggestions for hiking/ cycling tours in the area?	Vorschläge für Wanderungen/Radtouren in dieser Region? [for**shlay**guh fewr **van**deroongen/**rahd**tooren in **dee**zer reg**yon**]
Is the route	**Ist die Tour** [ist dee toor]
easy/difficult	leicht/schwer [liykht/shvair]
well marked	gut markiert [goot mar**keert**]
suitable for children?	für Kinder geeignet? [fewr **kin**der ge-**iyg**net]
How long will it take?	Wie lange dauert es? [vee **la**nguh **dow**ert es]
Where can I get a mountain guide?	Wo finde ich einen Bergführer? [voh **fin**duh ikh **iy**nen **bairg**fewrer]
How far is it to ...?	Wie weit ist es noch bis ...? [vee viyt ist es nokh bis]

Courses

I'd like to attend	**Ich möchte ... belegen.** [ikh **merkh**tuh be**lay**gen]
a language course	einen Sprachkurs [**iy**nen **shprakh**koors]
a cookery/painting course	einen Koch-/Malkurs [**iy**nen **kokh-/mahl**koors]
a dance workshop	einen Tanzworkshop [**iy**nen **tants**workshop]
a theatre workshop.	einen Theaterworkshop [**iy**nen tay**ah**terworkshop]
Are there still places available?	Sind noch Plätze frei? [zint nokh **ple**tsuh friy]
Where does the course/ the seminar take place?	Wo findet der Kurs/das Seminar statt? [voh **fin**det dair koors/das semi**nahr** shtat]
How many people are taking part in the course?	Wie viele Teilnehmer hat der Kurs? [vee **feel**uh **tiyl**naymer hat dair koors]
When does the course start?	Wann beginnt der Kurs? [van be**gint** dair koors]
How much is the course?	Wie viel kostet der Kurs? [vee feel **kos**tet dair koors]
Do you have somebody to look after children?	Gibt es eine Kinderbetreuung? [gibt es **iy**nuh **kin**derbetroyoong]

Football

So that you can join in the football conversation, here is a collection of soccer terms:

corner Ecke [**ek**kuh]
defender Abwehrspieler [**ap**vayrshpeeler]
forward Stürmer [**shtewr**mer]
foul Foul [fowl]
free kick Freistoß [**friy**shtos]
goal Tor [tor]
goalkeeper Torwart [**tor**vart]
offside abseits [**ap**ziyts]
left wing Linksaußen [**links**owsen]
right wing Rechtsaußen [**rekhts**owsen]
pass Pass [pas]
penalty Elfmeter [elf**may**ter]
referee Schiedsrichter [**sheeds**rikhter]

Outside the Thalia Theatre in Hamburg

Entertainment

Cinema, theatre, opera and concerts

Whats on at the cinema tonight?	Welche Filme laufen heute Abend im Kino? [**vel**khuh **fil**muh **low**fen **hoy**tuh **ah**bent im **kee**no]
Is the film	**Ist der Film** [ist dair film]
dubbed	synchronisiert [**zoon**kroniseert]
shown in the original version with subtitles?	in Originalversion mit Untertiteln? [in origi**nal**vairsyon mit **oon**tertiteln]
When does ... start?	**Wann beginnt** [van be**gint**]
the show	die Vorstellung [dee **for**shteloong]
the concert	das Konzert [das kon**tsairt**]
the matinée (performance)	die Nachmittagsvorstellung [dee **nakh**mittahgsforshteloong]
the ballet performance	die Ballettaufführung [dee ba**let**owf-fewroong]
the cabaret	das Varietee [das varrye**tay**]
the opera/operetta	die Oper/Operette [dee **oh**per/ope**ret**tuh]
the musical	das Musical [das **mew**zical]
the play	die Theatervorstellung [dee tay**ah**terforshteloong]
What's on	**Was wird ... gespielt?** [vas veert ge**shpeelt**]
tonight/tomorrow night	heute Abend/morgen Abend [**hoy**tuh **ah**bent/**mor**gen **ah**bent]
this weekend	dieses Wochenende [**dee**zes **vo**khenenduh]
at the theatre	im Theater [im tay**ah**ter]
at the opera house?	in der Oper [in dair **oh**per]
Where do I get tickets?	Wo bekommt man Karten? [voh be**kommt** man **kar**ten]

At the theatre

Eingang entrance
Galerie gallery
Garderobe cloakroom
links left
Loge box
Mitte centre
Notausgang emergency exit
Parkett stalls
Platz seat
1./2. Rang dress/upper circle
rechts right
Reihe row

How much are they? — Wie viel kosten sie? [vee feel **kos**ten zee]

Are there still tickets at the box office? — Gibt es noch Karten an der Abendkasse? [gibt es nokh **kar**ten an dair **ah**bent**kas**suh]

Are there special rates — **Gibt es verbilligte Karten** [gibt es fair**bil**ligtuh **kar**ten]
for children — für Kinder [fewr **kin**der]
for students — für Studenten [fewr shtoo**den**ten]
for senior citizens? — für Senioren? [fewr sen**yor**en]

* Ausverkauft. [**ows**fairkowft] — Sold out.

Two tickets/seats for . . ., please. — **Bitte zwei Karten/Plätze für** [**bit**tuh tsviy **kar**ten/**ple**tsuh fewr]
the show — die Vorstellung [dee **for**shteloong]
the concert — das Konzert [das kon**tsairt**]
tonight — heute Abend [**hoy**tuh **ah**bent]
tomorrow night — morgen Abend [**mor**gen **ah**bent]
at 8 o'clock — um zwanzig Uhr. [oom **tvan**tsig oor]

When does the show start? — Wann fängt die Vorstellung an? [van fengt dee **for**shteloong an]

How long is it? — Wie lange dauert sie? [vee **la**nguh **dow**ert zee]

Nightlife

Is there . . . around here? — **Gibt es hier** [gibt es heer]
a discotheque — eine Diskothek [**iy**nuh disko**tayk**]
a place to dance — ein Tanzlokal [iyn **tants**lokahl]
a (nice) pub — eine (nette) Kneipe [**iy**nuh (**net**tuh) **kniy**puh]
a bar — eine Bar [**iy**nuh bar]
a casino — ein Spielcasino [iyn **shpeel**casino]

Is this seat taken? — Ist dieser Platz besetzt? [ist **dee**zer plats be**zetst**]

Could I see the wine list, please? — Die Getränkekarte, bitte. [dee ge**tren**kekartuh **bit**tuh]

Shall we — **Möchten Sie** [**merkh**ten zee]
dance — tanzen [**tan**tsen]
have a drink — etwas trinken [**et**vas **trin**ken]
get a bit of fresh air? — frische Luft schnappen? [**fri**shuh looft **shnap**pen]

This one's on me. — Ich lade Sie ein. [ikh **lah**duh zee iyn]

Can I walk you	**Darf ich Sie ... begleiten?** [darf ikh zee be**gliy**ten]
home	nach Hause [nahkh **how**suh]
to the hotel?	ins Hotel [ins ho**tel**]
Would you like to come to my place?	Möchten Sie noch mit zu mir kommen? [**merkh**ten zee nokh mit tsoo meer **kom**men]
Thank you for the nice evening. Goodbye./ See you tomorrow.	Vielen Dank für diesen schönen Abend. [**fee**len dank fewr **dee**zen **sher**nen **ah**bent] Auf Wiedersehen!/Bis morgen! [owf **vee**derzayen/bis **mor**gen]

Festivals and events

When does ... start?	**Wann beginnt** [van be**gint**]
the festival	das (Volks)Fest [das (**folks**)fest]
the parade/procession	der Umzug/die Prozession [dair **oom**tsoog/dee protses**syon**]
the show/performance	die Show/Darbietung? [dee show/**dahr**beetoong]
Where does the show take place?	Wo findet die Veranstaltung statt? [voh **fin**det dee fair**an**shtaltoong shtat]
Where do I get/How much are the tickets?	Wo bekomme ich/Was kosten die Karten? [voh be**kom**muh ikh/vas **kos**ten dee **kar**ten]

Entertainment

actor	Schauspieler [sh-**ow**shpeeler]
actress	Schauspielerin [sh-**ow**shpeelerin]
band	Band [bahnt]
bouncer	Türsteher [**tewr**shtayer]
box office	Kasse [**kas**suh]
chamber music	Kammermusik [**kam**mermoozik]
choir	Chor [kohr]
circus	Zirkus [**tsir**koos]
comedy	Komödie [kom**mer**dyuh]
conductor	Dirigent [diri**gent**]
dancer	Tänzer [**ten**tser] *m.*; Tänzerin *f.* [**ten**tserin]
director	Regisseur [resheess**er**]
folk concert	Folkloreabend [fol**klor**uhahbent]
interval	Pause [**pow**suh]
jazz concert	Jazzkonzert [**jazz**kontsairt]
open-air theatre	Freilichtbühne [**friy**likhtbewnuh]
opera glasses	Opernglas [**oh**pernglahs]
orchestra	Orchester [or**kes**ter]
play	spielen [**shpee**len]
pop music	Popmusik [**pop**moozik]
première	Premiere [prem**yair**uh]
singer	Sänger [**zeng**er] *m.*; Sängerin in *f.* [**zeng**erin]
stage	Bühne [**bew**nuh]
stage set	Bühnenbild [**bew**nenbilt]

Exotic wares at 'Harry's' in Hamburg

Shopping

General

Where can I get	**Wo gibt es/Wo bekomme ich** [voh gibt es/voh be**kom**muh ikh]
films	Filme [**film**uh]
papers	Zeitungen [**tsiy**toongen]
food?	Lebensmittel? [**lay**bensmittel]
Is there ... around here?	**Gibt es hier in der Nähe** [gibt es heer in dair **nay**uh]
a bakery	eine Bäckerei [**iy**nuh bekke**riy**]
a food store/supermarket	ein Lebensmittelgeschäft/einen Supermarkt [iyn **lay**bensmittelgesheft/**iy**nen **zoo**permarkt]
a butcher's shop	eine Metzgerei? [**iy**nuh **mets**geriy]
* Werden Sie schon bedient? [**vair**den zee shon be**deent**]	Are you being served?
* Kann ich Ihnen helfen? [kan ikh **ee**nen **hel**fen]	Can I help you?
I'm just looking, thanks.	Ich möchte mich nur umsehen. [ikh **merkh**tuh mikh noor **oom**zayen]
I'd like ..., please.	**Ich möchte bitte** [ikh **merkh**tuh **bit**tuh]
stamps	Briefmarken [**breef**marken]
suntan lotion	Sonnenmilch. [**zon**nenmilkh]
How much is this?	Wie viel kostet das? [vee feel **kos**tet das]
That's (too) expensive.	Das ist (zu) teuer. [das ist (tsoo) **toy**er]
I (don't) like that.	Das gefällt mir (nicht). [das ge**felt** meer (nikht)]
I'll take it.	Ich nehme es. [ikh **nay**muh es]

Do you have anything else/ cheaper/bigger/smaller?	Haben Sie etwas anderes/Preiswerteres/ Größeres/Kleineres? [**hah**ben zee **et**vas **an**deres/**priys**verteres/**grer**serus/**kliy**neres]
Can I	**Kann ich** [kan ikh]
pay by cheque/traveller's cheque/credit card	mit Scheck/Reisescheck/Kreditkarte bezahlen [mit shek/**riy**zuhshek/kre**dit**kartuh be**tsah**len]
exchange this?	das umtauschen? [das **oom**towshen]
Where's the nearest cash dispenser/ bank?	Wo ist der nächste Geldautomat/die nächste Bank? [voh ist dair **naykhs**tuh **gelt**owtomat/dee **naykhs**tuh bank]
* Noch etwas? [nokh etvas]	Anything else?
That's all, thanks.	Danke, das ist alles. [**dan**kuh das ist **al**les]
Could you pack it for me, please?	Können Sie mir das einpacken? [**ker**nen zee meer das **iyn**pakken]
Do you have a carrier bag?	Kann ich eine Tragetüte haben? [kan ikh **iy**nuh **trahg**uhtewtuh **hah**ben]

Groceries

* Was wünschen Sie? [vas **vewn**shen zee]	What can I get you?
I'd like/Could I have . . ., please?	**Ich möchte bitte** [ikh **merkh**tuh **bit**tuh]
a piece of . . .	ein Stück . . . [iyn shtewk]
100 grams of . . .	100 g . . . [**hoon**dert gram]
(half) a kilo of . . .	ein (halbes) Kilo . . . [iyn (**hal**buhs) **kee**lo]
a litre of . . .	einen Liter . . . [**iy**nen **lee**ter]
a tin/bottle of . . .	eine Dose/Flasche . . . [**iy**nuh **doh**zuh/**flash**uh]
Could I try some of this, please?	Kann ich davon probieren? [kann ikh da**fon** pro**bee**ren]
* Darf es etwas mehr sein? [darf es **et**vas mayr ziyn]	It's a bit over. Is that all right?
A bit more/less, please.	Etwas mehr/weniger, bitte. [**et**vas mair/**vay**niger **bit**tuh]
It's all right.	Lassen Sie es so. [**las**sen zee es zo]

Opening hours

Warenhäuser [**vah**renhoyzer] *(department stores)* and shopping malls in the big cities normally close at 8pm. In smaller towns and villages, however, shops may close at 6 or 6.30pm but may keep longer opening hours on Thursdays and Fridays. In the morning the hours vary from shop to shop. Some open at 9am, others at 10am. On Saturday, small shops are open from 8am to 1 or 2pm. Department stores close at 4pm. For the four Saturdays before Christmas the shops stay open until 6pm. There is normally no trading on Sundays; apart from bakeries the only shops likely to be open are those at railway stations.

Groceries

baby food — Babynahrung [**ba**bynahroong]
(alcohol-free) beer — (alkoholfreies) Bier [(alko**hol**friyes) beer]
biscuits — Kekse [**kek**zuh]

cake — Kuchen [**koo**khen]
chocolate — Schokolade [shokko**lah**duh]
without colouring — ohne Farbstoffe [**oh**nuh **farb**shtoffuh]
cream — Sahne [**zah**nuh]

eggs — Eier [**iy**er]

fish — Fisch [fish]
flour — Mehl [mayl]
fruit — Obst [opst]

juice — Saft [zaft]

ketchup — Ketschup [**ket**chup]

margarine — Margarine [marga**ree**nuh]
mayonnaise — Majonäse [miyo**nay**zuh]
meat — Fleisch [fliysh]
full-cream milk — Vollmilch [**fol**milkh]
semi-skimmed milk — fettarme Milch [**fet**tarmuh milkh]
mustard — Senf [zenf]

nuts — Nüsse [**new**suh]

oil — Öl [erl]

pepper — Pfeffer [**pfef**fer]
porridge oats — Haferflocken [**hah**ferflokken]
without preservatives — ohne Konservierungsstoffe [**oh**nuh konsair**vee**roongs-shtoffuh]

rusk — Zwieback [**tsvee**bak]

salami — Salami [za**lah**mi]
salt — Salz [zalts]
spices — Gewürze [ge**vewr**tsuh]
sugar — Zucker [zooker]

tinned foods — Konserven [kon**zair**ven]

vinegar — Essig [**es**sig]
vegetables — Gemüse [ge**mew**zuh]

▶ **(See also food, page 44)**

Fruit and vegetables

apple — Apfel [**ap**fel]
apricot — Aprikose [apri**koh**zuh]
aubergine — Aubergine [obair**shee**nuh]
avocado — Avokado [avo**ka**do]

banana	Banane [ba**nah**nuh]
basil	Basilikum [ba**zi**likoom]
(runner/haricot/kidney) beans	(grüne/weiße/rote) Bohnen [**grew**nuh/**wiy**suh/**roh**tuh) **boh**nen]
broccoli	Brokkoli [**brok**koli]
cabbage	Kohl [kohl]
carrots	Karotten [ka**rot**ten]
cherries	Kirschen [**kir**shen]
chickpeas	Kichererbsen [**kik**kherairbsen]
chicory	Chicorée [**shi**kkoray]
chilli	Peperoni [peppe**ro**ni]
courgettes	Zucchini [**tsoo**kheeni]
cucumber	Gurke [**goor**kuh]
dates	Datteln [**dat**teln]
figs	Feigen [**fiy**gen]
garlic	Knoblauch [**knohb**lowkh]
grapes	Trauben [**trow**ben]
hazelnut	Haselnuss [**hahz**elnoos]
kiwi	Kiwi [**kee**vi]
leek	Lauch [lowkh]
lemon	Zitrone [tsi**troh**nuh]
lettuce	Kopfsalat [**kopf**zalaht]
mandarin orange	Mandarine [manda**ree**nuh]
mango	Mango [**man**go]
melon	Melone [me**loh**nuh]
olives	Oliven [o**lee**ven]
onion	Zwiebel [**tsvee**bel]
orange	Orange [o**ran**shuh]
parsley	Petersilie [payter**zee**lyuh]
peach	Pfirsich [**pfeer**sikh]
peanuts	Erdnuss [**aird**noos]
pear	Birne [**beer**nuh]
peas	Erbsen [**airp**zen]
pepper	Paprikaschote [paprika**shoh**tuh]
pineapple	Ananas [ana**nas**]
plum	Pflaume [**pflow**muh]
potatoes	Kartoffeln [kar**tof**feln]
raspberries	Himbeeren [**him**bairen]
spinach	Spinat [shpi**naht**]
strawberries	Erdbeeren [**aird**bairen]
sweetcorn	Mais [miys]
tomato	Tomate [to**mah**tuh]
turnips	Rüben [**rew**ben]
watermelon	Wassermelone [**va**sserme**loh**nuh]

Some common clothing items

anorak	Anorak [**an**orak]
belt	Gürtel [**gewr**tel]
bikini	Bikini [bi**kee**ni]
boots	Stiefel [**shtee**fel]
bra	BH [bay har]
cap	Mütze [**mew**tsuh]
gloves	Handschuhe [**hant**shoo-uh]
hat	Hut [hoot]
leggings	Leggings [**leg**gings]
knickers	Slip [slip]
sandals	Sandalen [zan**dah**len]
scarf	Schal [shahl]
sunhat	Sonnenhut [**zon**nenhoot]
swimsuit	Badeanzug [**bah**duhantsoog]
swimming trunks	Badehose [**bah**duh-**hoh**zuh]
tie	Krawatte [kra**vat**tuh]
tights	Strumpfhose [**shtroompf**hohsuh]
tracksuit	Trainingsanzug [trainingsantsoog]
underpants	Unterhose [**oon**terhohzuh]
waistcoat	Weste [**ves**tuh]

Clothes and shoes

I'm looking for	**Ich suche** [ikh **zoo**khuh]
a blouse/a shirt	eine Bluse/ein Hemd [**iy**nuh **bloo**zuh/iyn hemt]
a t-shirt	ein T-Shirt [iyn **tee**-shirt]
a pair of trousers/a skirt/ a dress	eine Hose/einen Rock/ein Kleid [**iy**nuh **hoh**zuh/**iy**nen rock/iyn kliyt]
a sweater/a pullover	einen Pullover [**iy**nen pull**ohver**]
a jacket	eine Jacke [**iy**nuh **yak**kuh]
a cardigan	eine Strickjacke [**iy**nuh s**htrik**yakkuh]
underwear/socks	Unterwäsche/Socken [**oon**terveshuh/**zo**cken]
a raincoat	eine Regenmantel [**iy**nuh **ray**genmantel]
a pair of shoes/trainers for ladies/men/children.	Schuhe/Turnschuhe [**shoo**-uh/**turn**shoo-uh] für Damen/Herren/Kinder. [fewr **dah**men/**hair**en/**kin**der]
I take size 40/I take size 39.	Ich habe Größe 40/Schuhgröße 39. [ikh **hah**buh **grer**suh **feer**tsig/**shoo**grersuh **noyn**oont**driy**sig]
Could I try this on?	Kann ich das probieren? [kan ikh das pro**bee**ren]
Do you have a mirror?	Haben Sie einen Spiegel? [**hah**ben zee **iy**nen **shpee**gel]
It fits nicely./It doesn't fit.	Das passt gut./Das passt nicht gut. [das passt goot/das passt nikht goot]
I (don't) like this/the colour.	Das/Die Farbe gefällt mir (nicht). [das/dee **fahr**buh ge**felt** meer (nikht)]

I'll take it.	Ich nehme es. [ikh **nay**muh es]
Do you have other styles/ colours?	Gibt es noch andere Modelle/Farben? [gibt es nokh **an**deruh mo**del**luh/**fahr**ben]
It is	**Es ist** [es ist]
too big/small	zu groß/klein [tsoo gros/kliyn]
too long/short	zu lang/kurz [tsoo lang/koorts]
too tight/loose.	zu eng/weit. [tsoo eng/viyt]
Is this	**Ist das** [ist das]
real leather	echtes Leder [**ekh**tes **le**der]
cotton	Baumwolle [**bowm**volluh]
wool	Wolle [**vol**luh]
silk/linen?	Seide/Leinen? [**ziy**duh/**liy**nen]
Could you	**Können Sie** [**ker**nen zee]
alter this	das ändern [das **en**dern]
repair these shoes?	die Schuhe reparieren? [dee **shoo**-uh repa**ree**ren]
When will it/will they be ready?	Wann ist es/sind sie fertig? [van ist es/zint zee **fair**tig]

Laundry and dry cleaning

I'd like to have these things cleaned/washed.	Ich möchte das reinigen/waschen lassen. [ikh **merkh**tuh das **riy**nigen/**va**shen **las**sen]
How much is it?	Wie viel kostet das? [vee feel **kos**tet das]
When can I pick it up?	Wann kann ich es abholen? [van kan ikh es **ap**hohlen]

Jewellery and watches

My watch/my alarm clock doesn't work.	Meine Armbanduhr/Mein Wecker geht nicht. [**miy**nuh **arm**bantoor/miyn **vek**ker gayt nikht]
My necklace is broken.	Meine Kette ist kaputt. [**miy**nuh **ket**tuh ist kap**poot**]
Could you repair it?	Können Sie das reparieren? [**ker**nen zee das repa**ree**ren]

Shoe and clothing sizes

German, British and American clothing and shoe sizes are not the same. The table opposite shows a range of German sizes, and the figures in brackets are the corresponding English/ American sizes.

It is always best to try on any article before buying it, however, as sizes can vary.

Women's clothing: 34 (8/4), 36 (10/6), 40 (14/10), 44 (18/14), 48 (22/18)

Men's clothing: 46 (36), 48 (38), 50 (40), 52 (42), 54 (44), 56 (46)

Men's and women's shoes: (f) 36 (3/4½), 37 (4/5½), 38 (5/6½), 39 (6/7½), 40 (7/8½), 41 (8/9½); (m) 41 (8/8½), 42 (9/9½), 43 (10/10½), 44 (11/11½)

I'd like	**Ich hätte gerne** [ikh **het**tuh **gair**nuh]
a new battery	eine neue Batterie [**iy**nuh **noy**uh batte**ree**]
a bracelet	ein Armband [iyn **arm**bant]
a brooch	eine Brosche [**iy**nuh **brosh**uh]
some earrings/a ring.	Ohrringe/einen Ring. [**ohr**-ringuh/**iy**nen ring]

Is this	**Ist das** [ist das]
genuine silver/gold	echt Silber/Gold [**ekh**tuhs **zil**ber/gold]
a pecious stone	ein echter Stein [iyn **ekh**ter shtiyn]
silver-/gold-plated?	versilbert/vergoldet? [fair**zil**bert/fair**gol**det]

Books, stationery, newspapers

Do you sell	**Haben Sie** [**hah**ben zee]
English papers/magazines	englische Zeitungen/Illustrierte [**eng**lishuh **tsiy**toongen/iloos**treer**tuh]
postcards	Ansichtskarten [**an**zikhtskarten]
stamps	Briefmarken [**breef**marken]
writing paper	Briefpapier [**breef**papeer]
envelopes	Umschläge [**oom**shlayguh]
pens/pencils	Kugelschreiber/Stifte [**koo**gelshriyber/**stif**tuh]
English books	englische Bücher [**eng**lishuh **bew**kher]
glue/adhesive tape?	Klebstoff/Klebeband? [**klayb**shtoff/**klay**buhbant]

I'd like	**Ich hätte gerne** [ikh **het**tuh **gair**nuh]
a map of ...	eine Landkarte von ... [**iy**nuh **lant**kartuh fon]
a street map	einen Stadtplan [**iy**nen **shtat**plan]
a travel guide	einen Reiseführer [**iy**nen **riy**zuhfewrer]
a hiking map	eine Wanderkarte [**iy**nuh **van**derkartuh]
a German–English dictionary.	ein deutsch–englisches Wörterbuch. [iyn doych-**eng**lishes **ver**terbookh]

Electrical appliances and photography

I'm looking for/I need	**Ich suche/Ich brauche** [ikh **zoo**khuh/ikh **brow**khuh)
an adapter	einen Adapter [**iy**nen a**dap**ter]
a battery	eine Batterie [**iy**nuh batte**ree**]
for my Walkman	für meinen Walkman [fewr **miy**nen **valk**man]
for my camera	für meinen Fotoapparat [fewr **miy**nen **fo**to-appa**raht**]
for my video camera	für meine Videokamera [fewr **mi**ynuh **vi**deokamera]
for my radio.	für mein Radio. [fewr miyn **rahd**yo]
I'd like	**Ich hätte gerne** [ikh **het**tuh **gair**nuh]
a colour film	einen Farbfilm [**iy**nen **farb**film]
a black-and-white film	einen Schwarzweißfilm [**iy**nen shvarts**viys**film]
a slide film	einen Diafilm [**iy**nen **dee**yafilm]
with 24/36 exposures	mit vierundzwanzig/sechsundreißig Aufnahmen [mit **feer**oont-tsvantsig/ **zex**oontdriysig **owf**nahmen]
a video cassette	eine Videokassette [**iy**nuh **vee**deokassettuh]
a standard lens	ein Standardobjektiv [iyn shtan**dart**obyek**teef**]
a wide-angle lens	ein Weitwinkelobjektiv [iyn **viyt**vinkelobyek**teef**]
a telephoto lens	ein Teleobjektiv [iyn **te**le-obyek**teef**]
a zoom lens.	ein Zoomobjektiv. [iyn **zoom**obyek**teef**]
Could you . . ., please?	**Können Sie mir** [**ker**nen zee meer]
put the film in the camera	den Film einlegen [den film **iyn**laygen]
develop this film for me	diesen Film entwickeln [**dee**zen film ent**vik**eln]
I'd like 9 by 13 prints, please.	Ich hätte gerne Abzüge im Format neun mal dreizehn. [ikh **het**tuh **gair**nuh **ap**tsewguh im for**maht** noyn mal **driy**tsayn]
* Glänzend oder matt? [**glen**tsent oder matt]	Gloss or matt?
Do you do passport photos?	Machen Sie Passbilder? [**ma**khen zee **pass**bilder]
When will the prints be ready?	Wann sind die Abzüge fertig? [van zint dee **ap**tsewguh **fair**tig]
. . . doesn't work.	**. . . funktioniert nicht richtig.** [foonktsyo**neert** nikht **rikh**tig]
My camera	Mein Fotoapparat [miyn **fo**toaparaht]
My flash	Mein Blitzlicht [miyn **blits**likht]
My video camera	Meine Videokamera [**miy**nuh **vee**deokamera]
Could you have a look at it?/Can you repair it?	Können Sie einmal nachsehen?/ Können Sie das reparieren? [**ker**nen zee **iyn**mal **nakh**sayen/**ker**nen zee das repa**ree**ren]
When can I pick it up?	Wann kann ich sie abholen? [van kann ikh zee **ap**hohlen]

Souvenirs and art and crafts

I'm looking for	**Ich suche** [ikh **zoo**khuh]
a souvenir	ein Reiseandenken [**riy**zuhandenken]
ceramics; pottery	Keramik [ke**rah**mik]
modern	modern [mo**dairn**]
antique	antik [an**teek**]
traditional	volkstümlich [**folks**tewmlikh]
jewellery	Schmuck [shmook]
leather goods.	Lederwaren. [**lay**dervahren]
What's typical of	**Was ist typisch für** [vas ist **tew**pish fewr]
this town	diese Stadt [**dee**zuh shtat]
this area	diese Gegend [**dee**zuh **gay**gend]
this country?	dieses Land? [**dee**zuhs land]
Is this	**Ist dies** [ist deez]
handmade	handgemacht [**hant**gemakht]
genuine/antique	echt/antik [ekht/an**teek**]
made in this area?	aus der Region? [ows dair reg**yon**]

Optician

My glasses are broken.	Meine Brille ist kaputt. [**miy**nuh **bril**luh ist kap**poot**]
Can you repair them?	Können Sie sie reparieren? [**ker**nen zee zee rapa**ree**ren]
Can you let me have a substitute pair?	Können Sie mir eine Ersatzbrille geben? [**ker**nen zee meer **iy**nuh er**zats**brilluh **gay**ben]
When can I pick up the glasses?	Wann kann ich die Brille abholen? [van kann ikh dee **bril**luh **ap**hohlen]
I'm shortsighted/ longsighted.	Ich bin kurzsichtig/weitsichtig. [ikh bin **koorts**zikhtig/**viyt**zikhtig]
I have	**Ich habe** [ikh **hah**buh]
lost my glasses/a contact lens	meine Brille/eine Kontaktlinse verloren [**miy**nuh **bril**luh/**iy**nuh kon**takt**linzuh fair**lor**en]
plus/minus ... in the right eye, ... in the left eye.	rechts plus/minus ..., links ... [rekhts ploos/**meen**oos links]
I need	**Ich brauche** [ikh **brow**khuh]
a pair of sunglasses	eine Sonnenbrille [**iy**nuh **zon**nenbrilluh]
a spectacle case	ein Brillenetui [iyn **bril**lenetvee]
a pair of binoculars	ein Fernglas [iyn **fairn**glahs]
cleansing solution/rinsing solution	Reinigungslösung/Aufbewahrungslösung [**riy**nigoongslersoong/**owf**bevahroongslersoong]
for hard/soft contact lenses.	für harte/weiche Kontaktlinsen. [fewr **har**tuh/**viy**khuh kon**takt**linzen]

Hairdresser

I'd like to make an appointment for tomorrow/the day after tomorrow at 10 o'clock.	Ich möchte einen Termin vereinbaren für morgen/übermorgen um 10 Uhr. [ikh **merkh**tuh **iy**nen tair**meen** fair**iyn**baren fewr **mor**gen/**ew**bermorgen oom tsayn oor]
Is that possible?	Geht das? [gayt das]
Can you attend to me now?	Können Sie mich gleich bedienen? [**ker**nen zee mikh gliykh be**dee**nen]
. . . , please.	**Bitte** [**bit**tuh]
Just a cut	nur schneiden [noor **shniy**den]
Wash, cut and blow-dry	waschen, schneiden und föhnen [**va**shen, **shniy**den oont **fer**nen]
Very short	ganz kurz [gants koorts]
Not too short	nicht zu kurz [nikht tsoo koorts]
Just a trim	nur die Spitzen schneiden [noor dee **shpi**tsen **shniy**den]
Just a shave	nur rasieren [noor ra**zee**ren]
Could you trim my beard	den Bart stutzen [dayn bart **shtoo**tsen]
No hairspray	kein Haarspray. [kiyn **hahr**shpray]
I'd like	**Ich möchte** [ikh **mer**khtuh]
a perm	eine Dauerwelle [**iy**nuh **dow**ervelluh]
my hair tinted/dyed.	eine Tönung/Färbung. [**iy**nuh **ter**noong/**fair**boong]
Thanks. that's fine..	Danke, so ist es gut. [**dan**kuh zo ist es goot]

Chemist

I'd like	**Ich hätte gerne** [ikh **het**tuh **gair**nuh]
some plasters	Heftpflaster [**heft**pflaster]
some tissues	Papiertaschentücher [pa**peer-ta**shentewkher]
paper towels	Papierhandtücher [pa**peer-hant**-tewkher]
a hand/skin cream	eine Hand-/Hautcreme [**iy**ne **hant-/howt**craymuh]
a suntan lotion with protection factor 6/12	eine Sonnenmilch mit Lichtschutzfaktor sechs/zwölf [**iy**nuh **zon**nenmilkh mit **likht**shootsfaktor zex/tsvewlf]
some shampoo	ein Shampoo [iyn sham**poo**]
for normal/dry/greasy hair	für normales/trockenes/fettiges Haar [fewr nor**mah**luhs/**trok**kenuhs/**fet**tiguhs hahr]
for dandruff.	gegen Schuppen. [**gay**gen **shoo**pen]

Tobacconist

A packet/carton of . . . , please.	**Eine Schachtel/Stange . . ., bitte.** [**iy**nuh **shakh**tel/**shta**nguh **bit**tuh]
with/without filters	mit/ohne Filter [mit/**oh**nuh **fil**ter]
A packet/A tin of pipe tobacco, please.	Ein Päckchen/Eine Dose Pfeifentabak, bitte. [iyn **pek**-khen/**iy**nuh **do**zuh **pfiy**fentabak **bit**tuh]
A box of matches/A lighter, please.	Eine Schachtel Steichhölzer/Ein Feuerzeug, bitte. [**iy**nuh **shakh**tel **shtriykh**herltser/iyn **foyer**tsoyg **bit**tuh]

Chemist

aftershave lotion	Rasierwasser [ra**zeer**vasser]
baby oil	Babyöl [**bay**by-erl]
baby's bottle	Babyflasche [**bay**byflashuh]
body lotion	Körperlotion [**ker**perlotsyon]
brush	Bürste [**bew**rstuh]
comb	Kamm [kam]
condom	Kondom [Kon**dohm**]; Präservativ [prezairva**teef**]
cotton wool	Watte [**vat**tuh]
deodorant	Deodorant [deodo**rant**]
detergent	Waschmittel [**vash**mittel]
dishcloth	Spültuch [**shpewl**tookh]
dummy	Schnuller [**shnoo**ler]
elastic hairband	Haargummi [**hahr**goomi]
eye shadow	Lidschatten [**leed**shatten]
flannel	Waschlappen [**vash**lappen]
hairspray	Hairspray [**hahr**shpray]
insect repellent	Insektenschutzmittel [in**zekt**enshootsmittel]
lip salve	Lippenpflegestift [**lip**penpfleguhshtift]
lipstick	Lippenstift [**lip**penshtift]
mascara	Wimperntusche [**vim**perntooshuh]
mirror	Spiegel [**shpee**gel]
nail file	Nagelfeile [**nah**gelfiyluh]
nail scissors	Nagelschere [**nah**gelshairuh]
nappies	Windeln [**vin**deln]
perfume	Parfüm [par**fewm**]
powder	Puder [**poo**der]
razor-blade	Rasierklinge [ra**zeer**klinguh]
saftey pin	Sicherheitsnadel [**zi**kherhiyts**nah**del]
sanitary towels	Damenbinden [**dah**menbinden]
sewing kit	Nähzeug [**nay**tsoyg]
shaving foam	Rasierschaum [ra**zeer**showm]
shower gel	Duschgel [**doosh**gayl]
soap	Seife [**ziy**fuh]
sponge	Schwamm [shvam]
styling gel	Haargel [**hahr**gayl]
tampons	Tampons [**tam**pons]
toilet paper	Toilettenpapier [toi**let**tenpapeer]
toothbrush	Zahnbürste [**tsahn**bewrstuh]
toothpaste	Zahnpasta [**tsahn**pasta]
tweezers	Pinzette [pin**tset**tuh]
washing-up liquid	Spülmittel [**shpewl**mittel]

On duty at the Oktoberfest

Practical Information

Medical assistance

At the doctor's surgery

I need a doctor (urgently).	Ich brauche (schnell) einen Arzt. [ikh **brow**khuh (shnell) **iy**nen artst]
Please call an ambulance/a doctor.	Rufen Sie bitte einen Krankenwagen/einen Notarzt. [**roo**fen zee **bit**tuh **iy**nen **kra**nkenvahgen/**iy**nen **noht**artst]
Where can I find a (English-speaking)	**Wo finde ich einen (englischsprachigen)** [voh **fin**duh ikh **iy**nen (**eng**lishshprahkhigen)]
doctor/dentist	Arzt/Zahnarzt [artst/**tsahn**artst]
gynaecologist	Frauenarzt [**frow**enartst]
paediatrician?	Kinderarzt? [**kin**derartst]
Can the doctor come here?	Kann der Arzt herkommen? [kann dair artst **hair**komen]
What are the surgery hours?	Wann hat er Sprechstunde? [van hat air **shprekh**shtoonduh]
Can I have an appointment immediately?	Kann ich gleich in die Praxis kommen? [kann ikh gliykh in dee **pra**xis **kom**men]
Can I wait?	Kann ich hier bleiben? [kann ikh **heer**bliyben]
When can I come?	Wann kann ich kommen? [van kann ikh **kom**men]
* Was fehlt Ihnen? [vas faylt **ee**nen]	What can I do for you?
I feel sick/faint (all the time).	Mir ist (ständig) schlecht/schwindlig. [meer ist (**shten**dig) shlekht/**shvin**delig]
I had a fall (and my head hurts).	Ich bin gestürzt (und mein Kopf tut weh). [ikh bin ge**shtewrtst** (oont miyn kopf toot veh)]

I've got	**Ich habe** [ikh **hah**buh]
a cold	mich erkältet [mikh air**kel**tet]
an allergy	eine Allergie [**iy**nuh alair**gee**]
diarrhoea	Durchfall [**doorkh**fal]
the flu/a cough	Grippe/Husten [**grip**puh/**hoos**ten]
a headache	Kopfschmerzen [**kopf**shmairtsen]
stomachache	Bauchschmerzen [**bowkh**shmairtsen]
earache	Ohrenschmerzen [**ohr**enshmairtsen]
a sore throat	Halsschmerzen [**hals**-shmairtsen]
cystitis	eine Blasenentzündung [**iy**nuh **bla**zenen**tsewn**doong]
shooting pains in the heart	Herzstechen [**hairts**-shtekhen]
a (high) temperature.	(hohes) Fieber. [(**ho**-uhs) **fee**ber]

* Seit wann haben Sie Fieber? [ziyt van **hah**ben zee **fee**ber]	When did the fever start?
2 days ago.	Seit zwei Tagen. [ziyt tsviy **tah**gen]
* Wo tut es weh? [vo toot es vay]	Where does it hurt?
* Es ist nichts schlimmes [es ist nikhts **shlim**mes]	It's nothing serious.
Is the leg/the arm/the finger broken?	Ist das Bein/der Arm/der Finger gebrochen? [ist das biyn/dair arm/dair **fin**ger ge**brok**khen]
I'm allergic to penicillin.	Ich bin allergisch gegen Penicillin. [ikh bin a**lair**gish **gay**gen penitsi**leen**]

I'm	**Ich bin** [ikh bin]
(4 months) pregnant	(im vierten Monat) schwanger [(im **feer**ten **moh**nat) **shva**nger]
diabetic	Diabetiker [deeya**bay**tiker]
chronically ill.	chronisch krank. [**kroh**nish krank]

I'm taking medication.	Ich nehme regelmäßig Medikamente. [ikh **nay**muh **re**gelmaysig medika**men**tuh]

Could you	**Können Sie mir** [**ker**nen zee meer]
prescribe this for me	das verschreiben [das fair**shriy**ben]
prescribe something for …, please?	etwas gegen … verschreiben? [**et**vas **gay**gen fair**shriy**ben]

Directions for use of medicine

vor/nach den Mahlzeiten	before/after food
in Wasser auflösen	dissolve in water
im Mund zergehen lassen	dissolve on the tongue
äußerlich/innerlich	external/internal
nüchtern	on an empty stomach
unzerkaut einnehmen	swallow whole
zwei-/dreimal täglich	twice/three times a day

At the dentist

I've got (terrible) toothache.	Ich habe (starke) Zahnschmerzen. [ikh **hah**buh (**shtar**kuh) **tsahn**shmairtsen]
I've lost a filling.	Ich habe eine Füllung verloren. [ikh **hah**buh **iy**nuh **few**loong fair**lor**en]
Could you see me immediately	**Können Sie** [**ker**nen zee] mich gleich behandeln [mikh gliykh be**han**deln]
give me something for the pain, please?	mir ein Schmerzmittel geben? [meer iyn **shmairts**mittel **gay**ben]
Could you do a temporary repair on the bridge/the crown/the inlay?	Bitte reparieren Sie die Brücke/Krone/das Inlay nur provisorisch. [**bit**tuh repa**ree**ren zee dee **brew**kuh/**kroh**nuh/das **in**lay noor provi**zoh**rish]
Could you give me a temporary filling?	Bitte machen Sie mir eine provisorische Füllung. [**bit**tuh **ma**khen zee meer **iy**nuh provi**zoh**rishuh **few**loong]

Medical assistance

Aids	Aids [aids]
allergy	Allergie [alair**gee**]
antibiotic	Antibiotikum [anti**byo**tikoom]
appendicitis	Blinddarmentzündung [**blin**darmen**tsewn**doong]
aspirin	Aspirin [aspi**reen**]
(strong) bleeding	(starke) Blutung [(**shtar**kuh) **bloo**toong]
burn	Verbrennung [fair**brenn**oong]
blood test	Bluttest [**bloot**-test]
certificate	Attest [at**test**]
circulatory problems	Kreislaufstörungen [**kriys**lowfshtewroongen]
cold	Erkältung [air**kel**toong]
concussion	Gehirnerschütterung [ge**hirn**air**shew**teroong]
condom	Kondom [kon**dohm**]
constipation	Verstopfung [fair**shtopf**oong]
cough mixture	Hustensaft [**hoos**tenzaft]
diabetes	Diabetes [deeya**bay**tes]
disinfectant	Desinfektionsmittel [desinfekts**yons**mittel]
eardrops	Ohrentropfen [**ohr**entropfen]
eyedrops	Augentropfen [**ow**gentropfen]
flu	Grippe [**grip**puh]
fracture	Bruch [brookh]
fungus (infection)	Pilz(infektion) [**pilts**(infektsyon)]
gastroenteritis	Magen-Darm-Erkrankung [**mah**gen-darm-air**krank**oong]
HIV-positive	HIV-positiv [hah ee fow **pos**iteef]
infection	Infektion [infekts**yon**]

Could you give me an injection, please?	Ich möchte eine Spritze. [ikh **merkh**tuh **iy**nuh **shpri**tsuh]
I'd rather not have an injection.	Ich möchte keine Spritze. [ikh **merkh**tuh **kiy**nuh **shpr**itsuh]
Is it bad?	Ist es schlimm? [ist es shlim]

At the hospital

Where is	**Wo ist** [voh ist]
the nearest hospital	das nächste Krankenhaus [das **naykh**ste **krank**enhows]
accident and emergency?	die Ambulanz? [dee amboo**lants**]
Please call	**Verständigen Sie bitte** [fair**shten**digen zee **bit**tuh]
Mr/Mrs ...	Herrn/Frau ... [hair/frow]
at the ... hotel.	im Hotel ... [im ho**tel**]

infectious	ansteckend [**an**shtekent]
inflammation	Entzündung [en**tsewn**doong]
migraine	Migräne [mig**ray**nuh]
ointment	Salbe [**zahl**buh]
operation	Operation [opairats**yon**]
painkiller	Schmerzmittel [**shmairts**mittel]
plaster	Pflaster [**pfla**ster]
poisoning	Vergiftung [fair**gift**oong]
pulled muscle	Muskelzerrung [**moos**keltsairoong]
pulled tendon	Sehnenzerrung [**zay**nentsairoong]
pus	Eiter [**iy**ter]
rash	Ausschlag [**ows**-shlahg]
seasickness	Seekrankheit [**zay**krankhiyt]
sleeping pills	Schlaftabletten [**shlaf**tabletten]
snakebite	Schlangenbiss [**shla**ngenbiss]
sprained	verstaucht [fair**shtowkht**]
sunstroke	Sonnenstich [**zon**nenshtikh]
temperature	Fieber [**fee**ber]
tranquilliser	Beruhigungsmittel [be**roo**-**ig**oongsmittel]
travel sickness	Reisekrankheit [**riy**zuhkrankhiyt]
vaccinate	impfen [**im**pfen]
vaccination	Impfung [**imp**foong]
virus	Virus [**vee**roos]
vomiting	Erbrechen [air**brek**khen]
wound	Wunde [**voon**duh]
X-ray	röntgen [**rernt**gen]

Do you have private/two-bed rooms?	Haben Sie Privat-/Zweibettzimmer? [**hah**ben zee pri**vaht**-/**tsviy**bet-tsimmer]
What's the diagnosis?	Wie ist die Diagnose? [vee ist dee deeya**gnoh**suh]
What kind of therapy is necessary?	Welche Therapie ist erforderlich? [**vel**khuh terra**pee** ist air**for**derlikh]
How long will I have to stay?	Wie lange muss ich bleiben? [vee **la**nguh moos ikh **bliy**ben]
(When) can I get up?	(Wann) darf ich aufstehen? [(van) darf ikh **owf**shtayen]
I (don't) feel (any) better.	Es geht mir (nicht) besser. [es gayt meer (nikht) **bes**ser]
I need	**Ich brauche** [ikh **brow**khuh]
a painkiller	ein Schmerzmittel [iyn **shmairts**mittel]
sleeping pills.	Schlaftabletten. [**shlaf**tbletten]
Am I well enough to travel?	Bin ich reisefähig? [bin ikh **riy**zuhfayig]
I'd like ..., please.	**Ich möchte** [ikh **merkh**tuh]
to see the doctor	den Arzt sprechen [dayn artst **shpre**khen]
to be discharged	entlassen werden [ent**las**sen **vair**den]
a medical report	einen Krankenbericht [**iy**nen **krank**enberikht]
a certificate	eine Bestätigung [**iy**ne be**shtay**tigoong]
for my medical insurance	für meine Versicherung [fewr **miy**nuh fair**zi**kheroong]
for my doctor.	für meinen Hausarzt. [fewr **miy**nen **hows**artst

At the pharmacy

I'm looking for a pharmacy.	Ich suche eine Apotheke. [ikh **zoo**khuh **iy**nuh apo**tay**kuh]
I have/I don't have a prescription.	Ich habe ein/Ich habe kein Rezept. [ikh **hah**buh iyn/ikh **hah**buh kiyn re**tsept**]
I need	**Ich brauche** [ikh **brow**khuh]
plaster	Heftpflaster [**heft**pflaster]
a painkiller	ein Schmerzmittel [iyn s**hmairts**mittel]
an insect repellent	ein Mückenmittel [iyn **mew**kenmittel]
something for a cough/ a headache/sunburn	etwas gegen Husten/Kopfschmerzen/ Sonnenbrand [**et**vas **ge**gen **hoos**ten/ (**kopf**shmairtsen/**zon**nenbrant]
for me	für mich [fewr mikh]
for adults	für Erwachsene [fewr air**vakh**senuh]
for children.	für Kinder. [fewr **kin**der]
Is this medicine strong?	Ist das Mittel stark? [ist das **mit**tel shtark]
How many tablets/drops do I have to take?	Wie viele Tabletten/Tropfen muss ich nehmen? [vee **fee**luh ta**blet**ten/**tro**pfen moos ikh **nay**men]
Please, give me a receipt/a copy of the prescription.	Geben Sie mir bitte eine Quittung/einen Durchschlag des Rezepts. [**gay**ben zee meer **bittu** **iy**nuh **kwitt**oong/**iy**nen **doorkh**shlahg des re**tsepts**]

Holidays and festivals

Is there a holiday today? — Ist heute Feiertag? [ist **hoy**tuh **fiy**ertahg]

What's being celebrated today? — Welches Fest wird heute gefeiert? [**vel**khes fest veert **hoy**tuh ge**fiy**ert]

Where are the most interesting parades? — Wo sind die interessantesten Umzüge? [voh zint dee interes**sant**esten **oom**tsewguh]

When does the festival start? — Wann beginnt das Festprogramm? [van be**gint** das **fest**program]

How long will it take? — Wie lange wird es dauern? [vee **lan**guh veert es **dow**ern]

Where does the festival take place? — Wo findet das Fest statt? [voh **fin**det das fest shtat]

Do we need/Where do we get tickets? — Brauchen wir/Wo bekommen wir Karten? [**brow**khen veer/voh be**kom**men veer **kar**ten]

How much are the tickets? — Wie viel kosten die Karten? [vee feel **kos**ten dee **kar**ten]

Money matters

Can I pay with ... here? — **Kann ich hier mit ... bezahlen?** [kan ikh heer mit be**tsah**len]

- traveller's cheques — Reiseschecks [**riy**suhsheks]
- my cheque card — meiner Scheckkarte [**miy**ner **shek**-kartuh]
- credit card — Kreditkarte [kre**dit**kartuh]

Where's the nearest — **Wo gibt es hier** [voh gibt es heer]

- bank — eine Bank [**iy**nuh bank]
- bureau de change — eine Wechselstube [**iy**nuh **ve**khselshtoobuh]
- post office — ein Postamt [iyn **post**amt]
- cash dispenser? — einen Geldautomaten? [**iy**nen **gelt**owtomahten]

It's easy to phone home

What are the opening hours?	Wie sind die Öffnungszeiten? [vee zint dee **erf**noongstsiyten]
What time does the bank close?	Wie lange hat die Bank geöffnet? [vee **lan**guh hat dee bank ge-**erf**net]
Where can I	**Wo kann ich hier** [voh kan ikh heer]
change some money	Geld wechseln [gelt **vekh**zeln]
cash a traveller's cheque?	einen Reisescheck einlösen? [**iy**nen **riy**suhshek **iyn**lerzen]
Can I have money transferred here from my bank?	Kann ich mir hier Geld von meiner Bank überweisen lassen? [kann ikh meer heer gelt fon **miy**ner bank ewber**viy**zen **la**ssen]
* Wie viel möchten Sie? [vee feel **merkh**ten zee]	How much do you want?
300 marks.	Dreihundert Mark. [**driy**hoondert mark]
What's the current exchange rate/the maximum amount per cheque?	Wie ist der aktuelle Wechselkurs/der Höchstbetrag pro Scheck? [vee ist dair aktoo-**el**luh v**ekh**zelkoors/dair **herkhst**betrahg pro shek]
What's the charge per cheque/per transfer?	Wie hoch ist die Gebühr pro Scheck/pro Überweisung? [vee hokh ist dee ge**bewr** pro shek/pro ewber**viy**zoong]
I'd like to change 400 pounds sterling/dollars into marks, please.	Ich möchte vierhundert Pfund/Dollar in Mark wechseln. [ikh **merkh**tuh **feer**hoondert pfoond/dollar in mark **vekh**zeln]
Please give me small notes/ some coins as well/ small change.	Geben Sie mir bitte kleine Scheine/auch Münzen/Kleingeld. [**gay**ben zee meer **bit**tuh **kliy**nuh **shiy**nuh/owkh **mewn**tsen/**kliyn**gelt]
Can I use my credit card to get cash?	Bekomme ich Bargeld mit meiner Kreditkarte? [be**kom**muh ikh **bar**gelt mit **miy**ner kre**dit**kartuh]
* Ihre Scheckkarte, bitte! [**ee**ruh **shek**-kartuh **bit**tuh]	Can I see your cheque card, please?
* Bitte unterschreiben Sie hier! [**bit**tuh oonter**shriy**ben zee heer]	Sign here, please.
Has my bank transfer/money order arrived yet?	Ist meine Banküberweisung/Postanweisung schon eingetroffen? [ist **miy**nuh **bank**ewber-viyzoong/**post**anviyzoong shohn **iyn**getroffen]

Crime and police

Where's the nearest police station?	Wo ist das nächste Polizeirevier? [voh ist das **naykh**stuh poli**tsiy**reveer]
Please call the police.	Rufen Sie bitte die Polizei! [**roo**fen zee **bit**tuh dee poli**tsiy**]
I've been	**Man hat mich** [man hat mikh]
robbed/swindled	bestohlen/betrogen [be**shtoh**len/be**troh**gen]
raped	vergewaltigt [fairge**val**tigt]
mugged.	überfallen. [ewber**fal**len]

This man is bothering/following me. — Dieser Mann belästigt/verfolgt mich. [**dee**zer man be**les**tigt/fair**folgt** mikh]

My car has been broken into. — Mein Auto ist aufgebrochen worden. [miyn **ow**to ist **owf**gebrokhen **vor**den]

... has been stolen. — **... ist gestohlen worden.** [ist ge**shtoh**len **vor**den]

- My passport — Mein Pass [miyn pas]
- My car/bicycle — Mein Auto/Fahrrad [miyn **ow**to/**far**-rahd]
- My wallet — Meine Brieftasche [**miy**nuh **breef**tashuh]
- My camera — Mein Fotoapparat [miyn **fo**toaparaht]
- My handbag — Meine Handtasche [**miy**nuh **hant**-tashuh]
- My cheques/cheque card — Mein Scheckheft/Meine Scheckkarte [miyn **shek**heft/**miy**nuh **shek**-kartuh]

I'd like to report — **Ich möchte ... anzeigen.** [ikh **merkh**tuh **an**tsiygen]

- a theft/robbery — einen Diebstahl/Überfall [**iy**nen **deeb**shtahl/**ew**berfal]
- a rape — eine Vergewaltigung [**iy**nuh fairge**val**tigoong]
- an accident. — einen Unfall [**iy**nen **oon**fal]

I'd like to — **Ich möchte** [ikh **merkh**tuh]

- speak to a lawyer — mit einem Anwalt sprechen [mit **iy**nem **an**valt **shpre**khen]
- call my embassy. — meine Botschaft anrufen. [**miy**nuh **boht**shaft an**roo**fen]

Does anyone here speak English? — Spricht hier jemand Englisch? [shprikht heer **yay**mand **eng**lish]

I need — **Ich brauche** [ikh **brow**khuh]

- an interpreter — einen Dolmetscher [**iy**nen **dol**metsher]
- a written document for insurance purposes. — eine Bescheinigung für die Versicherung. [**iy**nuh be**shiy**nigoong fewr dee fair**zi**kheroong]

It wasn't my fault. — Ich bin nicht schuld. [ikh bin nikht shoolt]

I've got nothing to do with it. — Damit habe ich nichts zu tun. [**da**mit **hah**buh ikh nikhts tsoo toon]

* Wann/Wo ist es passiert? [van/voh ist es pa**seert**] — When/Where did it happen?

* Wo wohnen Sie hier/in England? [voh **voh**nen zee heer/in **eng**lant] — What's your address here/in England?

Emergencies

* Achtung! [**akh**toong] — Caution!

* Notausgang [**noht**owsgang] — Emergency Exit

* Vorsicht, Lebensgefahr! [**for**zikht **lay**bensgefar] — Caution, danger!

Help! — Hilfe! [**hil**fuh]

Opening times

When does ... open/close?	**Wann öffnet/schließt** [van **erf**net/shleest]
the supermarket	der Supermarkt [dair **zoo**permarkt]
the department store	das Kaufhaus [das **kowf**hows]
the shop	das Geschäft [das ge**sheft**]
the bank	die Bank [dee bank]
the post office	das Postamt [das **post**amt]
the museum	das Museum [das moo**zay**-oom]
the pub	die Kneipe? [dee **kniy**puh]

Post office

Where can I find	**Wo ist hier bitte** [voh ist heer **bit**tuh]
a post office	die Post [dee post]
a postbox?	ein Briefkasten? [iyn **breef**kasten]
I'd like	**Ich möchte** [ikh **merkh**tuh]
10 stamps/ special issue stamps	zehn Briefmarken/Sondermarken [tsayn **breef**marken/**zon**dermarken]
for postcards/letters	für Karten/Briefe [fewr **kar**ten/**bree**fuh]
to England/to the USA	nach England/ in die USA [nakh **eng**lant/in dee oo es **ah**]
a phonecard.	eine Telefonkarte. [**iy**nuh tele**fon**kartuh]
By airmail, please.	Mit Luftpost, bitte. [mit **looft**post **bit**tuh]
Express, please.	Als Eilbrief, bitte. [als **iyl**breef **bit**tuh]
* Postlagernd. [**post**lagernt]	Poste restante.
Do you have any mail for me?	Ist Post für mich da? [ist post fewr mikh da]
My name is ...	Mein Name ist ... [miyn **nah**muh ist]
I would like to send a packet/parcel/a telegram.	Ich möchte ein Päckchen/ein Paket/ein Telegramm aufgeben. [ikh **merkh**tuh iyn **pek**-khen/iyn pak**kay**t/iyn tele**gram** **owf**geben]
How much do you charge for ten words?	Wie viel kosten zehn Wörter? [vee feel **kos**ten tsayn **ver**ter]
I'd like to make a phone call to England/the United States/Australia.	Ich möchte nach England/in die USA/nach Australien telefonieren. [ikh **merkh**tuh nakh **eng**lant/in dee oo es **ah**/nakh ows**tral**yen telefo**nee**ren]
Can I call directly?	Kann ich durchwählen? [kan ikh **doorkh**vaylen]

▶ **(See also telecommunications, page 82)**

Can I send a fax from here?	Kann ich hier ein Fax abschicken? [kann ikh heer iyn fax ap**shik**ken]
What do you charge for that?	Wie viel kostet das? [vee feel **ko**stet das]

Radio and television

On which wavelength can I pick up	**Auf welcher Frequenz kann man ... empfangen?** [owf **vel**kher fre**kwents** kann man em**pfang**en]
the traffic report	den Verkehrsfunk [den fair**kairs**foonk]
English radio programmes?	englische Radioprogramme? [**eng**lishuh **rah**dyoprogrammuh]
What time is the news?	Um wie viel Uhr gibt es Nachrichten? [um vee feel oor gibt es **nahkh**rikhten]
Do you have a TV guide?	Haben Sie ein Fernsehprogramm? [**hah**ben zee iyn **fairn**zayprogram]
What channels do you get?	Welche Programme sind zu empfangen? [**vel**khuh pro**gram**muh zint tsu em**pfang**en]

Telecommunications

(Where) can I	**(Wo) Kann ich hier** [(voh) kan ikh heer]
make a phone call	telefonieren [telefo**nee**ren]
buy a phonecard	eine Telefonkarte kaufen [**iy**nuh tele**fon**kartuh **kow**fen]
surf the Internet?	im Internet surfen? [im **in**ternet **zur**fen]
Is there ... here?	**Gibt es hier** [gibt es heer]
a phone box	eine Telefonzelle [tele**fon**tselluh]
a payphone/cardphone	ein Münztelefon/Kartentelefon [iyn **mewnts**telefon/**kar**tentelefon]
an Internet café	ein Internetcafé? [internetcaf**fay**]
Can you change this?	Können Sie bitte wechseln? [**ker**nen zee **bit**tuh **vekh**seln]
I need coins for the telephone.	Ich brauche Münzen zum Telefonieren. [ikh **brow**khuh **mewn**tsen tsoom telefo**nee**ren]
Can you give me	**Wie ist bitte** [vee ist **bit**tuh]
the country code/ local code for	die Landesvorwahl/Ortsvorwahl von [dee **lan**duhsforvahl/**orts**forvahl fon]
Great Britain	Großbritannien [**grohs**brittanyen]
Can I dial direct to ...?	Kann ich durchwählen nach ...? [kan ikh **doorkh**wayhlen nakh]
A long-distance call to ..., please.	Ein Ferngespräch nach ...! [iyn **fern**gespraykh nakh]
What's the charge per minute to ...?	Was kostet eine Minute nach ...? [vas **kos**tet iynuh mi**noo**tuh nakh]
Is there a cheap rate at night-time?	Gibt es einen günstigen Nachttarif? [gibt es **iy**nen **gewn**stigen **nakht**-tareef]
I'd like to make a reverse-charge call.	Ich möchte ein R-Gespräch anmelden. [ikh **merkh**tuh iyn **air**-geshpraykh **an**melden]
* Falsch verbunden. [falsh fair**boon**den]	Sorry, wrong number
There is no reply.	Es meldet sich niemand. [es **mel**det zikh **nee**mant]

Making phone calls

Most public telephones require **Telefonkarten** [tele**fon**karten] *(phonecards)* which are sold for DM12 or DM50 at post offices, newspaper stands and some other shops.

Private companies now offer phone calls at cheaper rates, but their systems are not always very convenient. Every town has its own dialling code and these are listed under the local network heading in the telephone directory. As elsewhere in Europe, the mobile phone or **Handy** [hendee] is catching on rapidly.

To phone England, prefix your number with 0044 and omit the zero from the local code. The code for Eire is 00353, the United States 001.

Hello! — Hallo! [huh**law**]
Who's calling? — Wer spricht? [vair shprikht]
This is ... — Hier spricht ... [heer shprikht]
Can I speak to Mr/Mrs ... ? — Kann ich Herrn/Frau ... sprechen? [kann ikh hairn/frow **shpre**khen]

* Am Apparat. [am apa**raht**] — Speaking.
* Er/Sie ist leider nicht da. [air/zee ist **liy**der nikht da] — He/She is not here at the moment.

Do you speak English? — Sprechen Sie Englisch? [**shpre**khen zee **eng**lish]
When can I reach him/her? — Wann ist er/sie zu sprechen? [van ist air/zee tsoo s**hpre**khen]
I'll call again later. — Ich rufe später wieder an. [ikh **roo**fuh **shpay**ter **vee**der an]
Please tell him/her that I called. — Richten Sie ihm/ihr bitte aus, dass ich angerufen habe. [**rikh**ten zee eem/eer **bit**tuh ows das ikh **an**geroofen **hah**buh]
My number is ... — Meine Nummer ist ... [**miy**nuh **noo**mer ist]
Thanks, goodbye. — Danke, auf Wiederhören. [**dan**kuh owf **vee**derheren]

Toilets

Where are the toilets please? — Wo sind die Toiletten, bitte? [voh zint dee toi**let**ten **bit**tuh]
Is there a public toilet around here? — Gibt es hier eine öffentliche Toilette? [gibt es heer **iy**nuh **er**fentlikhuh toi**let**tuh]

* Damen/Herren. [**dah**men/**hai**ren] — Ladies/Gentlemen.

Tipping

Is service included? — Ist der Service im Preis inbegriffen? [ist der **zer**vis im priys inbe**gri**ffen]
How much does one tip? — Wie viel Trinkgeld ist üblich? [vee feel **trink**gelt ist **ew**blikh]
That's for you. — Das ist für Sie! [das ist fewr zee]
Keep the change. — Behalten Sie den Rest! [be**hal**ten zee dayn rest]
That's fine. — Stimmt so! [shtimt zo]

English–German A–Z

A

accident Unfall [oonfal] 24
accommodation Unterkunft [oonterkoonft] 32
address Adresse [ad**dress**uh] 15
admission Eintritt [**iyn**tritt] 52, 57
adult Erwachsener [air**vakh**sener] 27
advance booking Vorverkauf [**for**fairkowf] 58
aeroplane Flugzeug [**floog**tsoyg] 28
age Alter [**al**ter] 14
aim Ziel [tseel]
air Luft [looft]
air bed Luftmatratze [**looft**matratsuh] 53, 60
air-conditioning Klimaanlage [**kli**ma-an**lah**guh] 38
airport Flughafen [**floog**hahfen] 28
alarm clock Wecker [**vek**ker] 66
all alle [**al**luh]
allowed erlaubt [air**low**pt] 23, 54
alone allein [a**liyn**]
ambulance Krankenwagen [**kran**ken**vah**gen] 72, 75
amount Betrag [be**trahg**] 43, 77
angry böse [**ber**zuh]
animal Tier [teer]
answering machine Anrufbeantworter [**an**roofbay**ant**vorter] 82
antiques Antiquitäten [anteekwi**tay**ten] 69
appointment Verabredung [fair**ap**raydoong]
area code Vorwahl [for**vahl**] 82
arm Arm [arm] 73
arrival Landung [**lan**doong] 28, 29
art gallery Kunstgalerie [**koonst**galeree] 50
arts and crafts Kunsthandwerk (Pl) [**koonst**handvairk] 69
at home daheim [da**hiym**]
at least wenigstens [**vay**nigstens]
attention Achtung! [**akh**toong] 23, 54
aunt Tante [**tan**tuh] 13
Austria Östereich [**er**striykh]
autumn Herbst [hairbst] 19

B

baby Baby [**bay**by]
baby bottle Babyflasche [**bay**byflashuh] 71
bachelor Junggeselle [yoong-ge**zel**luh] 14
backpack Rucksack [**rook**sak] 55
bad schlecht [shlekht]
bag Tüte [**tew**tuh] 60
bakery Bäckerei [bekke**riy**] 60
ball Ball [bal] 55
bank Bank [bank] 77
bank *(river)* Ufer [**oo**fer] 53
bath Bad [baht] 32, 53
battery Batterie [batte**ree**] 26, 66
bay Bucht [bookht] 53, 55
beach Strand [shtrand] 53
beach umbrella Sonnenschirm [**zon**nensheerm] 53
beautician Kosmetiksalon [kos**may**tikzalohn]
beautiful hübsch [hewbsh]
bed and breakfast Pension [pens**yon**] 32, 39
bed Bett [bet] 38
beer Bier [beer] 48
beginning Anfang [**an**fang] 57
behind hinter [**hin**ter]
belt Gürtel [**gew**rtel] 64
between zwischen [**tsvi**shen]
bicycle Fahrrad [**far**-rahd] 22, 23
big groß [grohs]
bikini Bikini [bi**kee**ni] 64
bill Rechnung [**rekh**noong] 43
birthday Geburtstag [ge**boorts**tahg] 14
blanket Decke [**dek**kuh] 34
blood Blut [bloot] 74
blouse Bluse [**bloo**zuh] 64
boat Boot [boht] 53
boiled gekocht [ge**kokht**]
book(shop) Buch(handlung) [**bookh**-handloong] 66
boots Stiefel [**stee**fel] 64
border Grenze [**gren**tsuh] 21
boring langweilig [**lang**viylig]
born geboren [ge**boh**ren]
boss Chef [shef]
both beide [**biy**duh]

bottle Flasche [**fla**shuh]
bottle opener Flaschenöffner [**fla**shenerfner] 60, 61
boutique Boutique [boo**teek**] 64
bowl Schüssel [**shlew**sel] 38
boy Junge [**yoo**nguh] 64
boyfriend Freund [froynt] 13
bra BH [bay **har**] 64
breakfast Frühstück [**frew**shtewk] 34, 44
bridge Brücke [**brew**kuh] 50
bring mitbringen [**mit**bringen]
broken kaputt [kap**poot**]
brooch Brosche [**bro**shuh] 66
brother Bruder [**broo**der] 13
brother-in-law Schwager [**shvah**ger] 13
bureau de change Wechselstube [**vekh**zelstoobuh] 77, 78
bus (station) Bus(bahnhof) [**boos**bahnhof] 27, 28
butcher's shop Metzgerei [metsge**riy**] 60
button Knopf [knopf]
buy kaufen [**kow**fen]

C

cabin Kabine [ka**bee**nuh] 29
café Café [kaf**fay**] 40
calm Ruhe [**roo**-uh]
camera Fotoapparat [fotoapa**raht**] 66, 78
camper van Wohnmobil [**vohn**mobeel] 37, 39
camping site Campingplatz [**cam**pingplats] 37
cap Mütze [**mew**tsuh] 64
car Auto [**ow**to] 22, 24, 26
car park Parkplatz [**park**plats]
caravan Wohnwagen [**vohn**vahgen] 37
cash Bargeld [**bahr**gelt] 77
cash desk Kasse [**kas**suh] 57, 60
castle Burg [boorg] 50
cat Katze [**ka**tsuh] 35
cathedral Kathedrale [katay**drah**luh] 51
cause Ursache [**oor**zakhuh]
celebration Feier [**fiy**er] 77
centimetre Zentimeter [tsenti**may**ter] 17
centre Zentrum [**tsen**troom] 22
ceramics Keramik [ke**rah**mik] 66
certificate Bescheinigung [be**shiy**nigoong]
chain Kette [**ket**tuh]
chair Stuhl [shtool]
chapel Kapelle [ka**pel**luh] 51
charter flight Charterflug [charter**floog**] 28
cheap billig [**bil**lig]
chemist Drogerie [droge**ree**] 70, 71
cheque Scheck [shek] 77, 79
child Kind [kint] 27, 41
church Kirche [keerkhuh] 50
cigarette Zigarette [tsiga**ret**tuh] 70
cinema Kino [keeno] 57
city Stadt [shtat] 50
city centre Stadtzentrum [shtat-**tsen**troom] 50
clean sauber [**zow**ber]
clear klar [klar]
close nahe [**nah**-uh]
closed geschlossen [ge**shlos**sen] 81
clothing Kleidung [**kliy**doong] 61, 64
cloud Wolke [**vol**kuh] 18
coach Reisebus [**riy**zuhboos]
coast Küste [**kews**tuh] 53
coat Mantel [**man**tel] 64
coin Münze [**mewn**tsuh] 39, 77, 82
cold kalt [kalt]
collar Kragen [**krah**gen] 64
colour Farbe [**far**buh] 20, 64
comb Kamm [kamm] 70, 71
come back wiederkommen [**vee**derkommen]
come in herein! [hair**iyn**]
company Firma [**feer**ma]
compartment Abteil [ap**tiyl**] 27
complaint Beschwerde [be**shvair**duh] 42
concert Konzert [kon**tsairt**] 57
condom Kondom [kon**dohm**]; Präservativ [prezairva**teef**] 71, 75
conductor Schaffner [**shaf**fner] 27, 29
congratulate gratulieren [gratoo**lee**ren] 14
connecting (flight/train) Anschluss (flug/-zug) [anshloos (**floog**/-**tsoog**)]
consulate Konsulat [konsoo**laht**] 22, 79
contraceptive Verhütungsmittel [fair**hew**toongsmittel] 76
contract Vertrag [fair**trahg**]
convent Kloster [**kloh**ster] 51
cook Koch (m.) [kokh]; Köchin (f.) [**ker**khin] 40
cooked gekocht [ge**kokht**]

corksrew Korkenzieher [korken**tsee**-er] 60
corner Ecke [**ek**kuh] 22, 56
cottage Ferienhaus [fairyen**hows**] 35
cotton Baumwolle [bowm**vol**luh] 65
cotton buds Wattestäbchen [**vat**tuh**shteb**khen] 71
cotton wool Watte [**vat**tuh] 71
couchette Liegewagen [**lee**guhvahgen] 27, 29
counter Schalter [**shal**ter]
country Land [lant]
country road Landstraße [**lant**shtrasuh] 24
cousin Cousin (m.) [koo**za**]; Cousine (f.) [koo**zee**nuh] 13
credit card Kreditkarte [kre**dit**kartuh] 77
cruise Kreuzfahrt [**croyts**faht] 29
cry weinen [**viy**nen]
cup Tasse [**tas**suh] 42
currency Währung [**vair**oong] 77
cushion Kissen [**kis**sen]
customs Zoll [tsol] 21
cutlery Besteck [be**shtek**] 38, 42

D

damp feucht [foykht]
dance tanzen [**tan**tsen] 58
danger Gefahr [ge**fahr**] 23, 54
dark dunkel [**doon**kel] 20
date Datum [**da**toom] 19
date Verabredung [fair**ap**raydoong] 15, 16
daughter Tochter [**tokh**ter] 13
day Tag [tahg] 19
day ticket Tageskarte [**tah**geskartuh] 44
deckchair Liegestuhl [**lee**guhshtool] 53
deep tief [teef]
degree Grad [grahd] 16, 72
delicacy Delikatesse [delika**tes**suh] 44
dentist Zahnarzt [**tsahn**artst] 74
department store Kaufhaus [**kowf**hows] 60
dessert Nachtisch [**nahkh**tish] 47
destination Reiseziel [**riy**zuhtseel]
detergent Waschmittel [**vash**mittel] 71
die sterben [**shtair**ben]
diesel Diesel [**dee**zel] 24
difference Unterschied [**oon**tersheet]
different anders [**an**ders]; verschieden [fair**shee**den]
difficult schwierig [**shvee**rig]
dinner Abendessen [**ah**bentessen]
direct flight Direktflug [dee**rekt**floog] 28
direct(ly) direkt [dee**rekt**]
direction Richtung [**rikh**toong] 22, 27
director Direktor [dee**rek**tor] 32, 57
dirty schmutzig [**shmoo**tsig]
discotheque Diskothek [disko**tayk**] 58
discount Rabatt [ra**bat**] 60
dish Gericht [ge**rikht**] 40, 44
disturb stören [**shter**en]
diversion Umleitung [**oom**liytoong] 23
dizzy schwindlig [**shvin**dlig] 72
doctor Arzt [artst] 72
dog Hund [hoond] 35, 54
door Tür [tewr] 38
double doppelt [**dop**pelt]
doubt Zweifel [**tsviy**fel]
dress Kleid [kliyt] 64
drink *(n.)* Getränk [ge**trenk**] 48
drink *(v.)* trinken [**trin**ken] 40, 42, 48
drinking water Trinkwasser [**trink**vasser] 29
driver Fahrer [**far**er] 27, 31
driving licence Führerschein [**few**rershiyn] 21
dry trocken [**trok**ken]
dry cleaning Reinigung [**riy**nigoong] 39, 65
dummy Schnuller [**shnoo**ler] 71

E

early früh [frew]
earrings Ohrringe [**ohr**-ringuh] 66
East Osten [**os**ten] 22
easy leicht [liykht]
edible essbar [**ess**bar]
education Erziehung [air**tsee**-oong]
electrical shop Elektrohandlung [e**lek**trohandloong] 66
electricity Strom [shtrohm] 39, 66
embassy Botschaft [**boht**shaft] 22, 79
emergency exit Notausgang [**noht**owsgang] 58
empty leer [layr]
engaged *(telephone)* belegt [be**laygt**]
engine Motor [mo**tor**] 25, 26
England England [**eng**lant] 13
English englisch [**eng**lish] 13, 40
entrance Eingang [**iyn**gang] 58
environment Umwelt [**oom**velt] 55

environmental protection Umweltschutz [**oom**veltshoots] 55
estate Landgut [**lant**goot]
evening Abend [**ah**bent] 20
event Veranstaltung [fair**an**shtaltoong] 57, 77
events guide Veranstaltungskalender [fair**an**shtaltoongskal**en**der] 49, 77
excuse me Verzeihung! [fair**tsiy**oong] 13
exhausted erschöpft [air**sher**pft]
exhausting anstrengend [**an**shtrengent]
exit Ausfahrt [**ows**fahrt]: Ausgang [**ows**gang] 27, 58
expenses Unkosten [**oon**kosten]
expensive teuer [**toy**er]
extend verlängern [fair**leng**ern]
extra charge Zuschlag [**tsoo**shlag] 27, 30

F

factory Fabrik [fa**breek**]
faithful treu [troy]
family Familie [fa**meel**yuh] 13, 38
fashion Mode [**moh**duh] 64
fat dick [dik]
father Vater [**fah**ter] 13
fault Schuld [shoolt] 78
faulty defekt [de**fekt**]
fax Telefax [tele**fax**] 35, 82
fear Angst [angst] 78
fee Gebühr [ge**bewr**] 77
ferry Fähre [**fair**uh] 29
few wenige [**vay**niguh]
field Feld [felt]
film Film [film] 57, 67
finally endlich [**end**likh]
fine Geldstrafe [**gelt**shtrahfuh] 78
finger Finger [**fin**ger] 73
finished fertig [**fair**tig]
fire (extinguisher) Feuer(löscher) [**foy**er(**ler**sher)] 79
fire brigade Feuerwehr [**foy**ervair] 79
firm fest [fest]
fishmonger Fischgeschäft [**fish**gesheft] 45
flat Wohnung [**voh**noong] 35
flea market Flohmarkt [**floh**markt] 60, 69
flight Flug [floog] 28
flight attendant Steward *(m.)* [**stoo**-ard]; Stewardess *(f.)* [stoo-ar**dess**]
flirt flirten [**flir**ten]
floor Boden [**boh**den]; Stockwerk [**shtok**vairk] 32
flower (shop) Blumen(laden) [**bloo**men(lahden)] 60
fly Fliege [**flee**guh]
food Essen [**ess**en] 40
foot Fuß [foos] 73
football Fußball [**foos**bal] 54, 56
for für [fewr]
foreigner Ausländer [**ows**lender] 15
forest Wald [valt] 55
forget vergessen [fair**gess**en]
fork Gabel [**gah**bel] 42
form Formular [formoo**lar**] 21
fragile zerbrechlich [tsair**brekh**likh]
free frei [friy]
fresh frisch [frish]
Friday Freitag [**friy**tahg] 19
fruit Obst [opst] 60, 62
full voll [foll]; *(food)* satt [zat]
full board Vollpension [**foll**pensyon] 33
fun Spaß [shpas] 57
furious wütend [**vew**tent]
furniture (shop) Möbel(geschäft) [**mer**bel(ges**heft**)] 60

G

garage *(parking)* Garage [ga**rah**shuh] 38; *(repair)* Werkstatt [**vairk**shtat] 25
garden Garten [**gar**ten] 50
gentleman Herr [hair]
genuine echt [ekht]
German deutsch [doych]
Germany Deutschland [**doych**lant]
girl Mädchen [**mayd**khen] 64
girl friend Freundin [**froyn**din] 13
give my regards to... Schöne Grüße an... [**sher**nuh **grew**suh an] 12
gladly gern [gairn]
glass Glas [glahs] 42, 50
glasses Brille [**bril**luh] 69
gloves Handschuhe [**hant**shoo-uh] 64
go gehen [**gay**en]
good gut [goot]
goodbye Abschied [**ap**sheet] 35
government Regierung [re**geer**oong]
gram(s) Gramm [gram] 18, 61
grandchild Enkelkind [**en**kelkint] 13
grandfather Großvater [**grohs**fahter] 13
grandmother Großmutter [**grohs**mooter] 13
greet grüßen [**grew**sen]

groceries Lebensmittel [**le**bensmittel] 60, 62
ground Fußboden [**foos**bohden]
group Gruppe [**groo**puh]
guided tour Führung [**few**roong] 49, 52

H

hair(brush) Haar(bürste) [**hahr**(bewrstuh)] 71
hairdresser Friseur [free**zur**] 70
half halb [halp]
hall Saal [zahl]
hand luggage Handgepäck [**hant**gepek] 28
handbag Handtasche [**hant**-tashuh] 69, 78
happy glücklich [**glewk**likh]
harbour Hafen [**hah**fen] 29, 50
hard hart [hart]
hat Hut [hoot] 64
have haben [**hah**ben]
head Kopf [kopf] 72, 73
healthy gesund [ge**zoont**]
heating Heizung [**hiy**tsoong] 34, 38
heavy schwer [shvair]
help! Hilfe! [**heel**fuh] 79
high hoch [hohkh]
hobby Hobby [**hob**by]
holiday Feiertag [**fiy**ertahg] 77; Urlaub [**oor**lowb]
holidays Ferien [**fair**yen]
home country Heimat [**hiy**mat]
home-made hausgemacht [**hows**gemakht]
hope hoffen [**hof**fen]
hospital Krankenhaus [**kra**nkenhows] 75
hot heiß [hiys]
hour Stunde [**stoon**duh] 18, 20
house Haus [hows] 35, 50
hunger Hunger [**hoo**nger] 40
hurt verletzt [fair**letst**]
husband Ehemann [**eh**uhman] 13
hut Hütte [**hew**tuh] 35

I

identity card Personalausweis [pairso**nahl**owsviys] 21, 78
if wenn [ven]
ill krank [krank] 72
important wichtig [**vikh**tig]
in charge zuständig [**tsoo**shtendig]
included inklusiv [inkloo**zeef**]
information Auskunft [**ows**koonft] 49
inhabitant Einwohner [**iyn**vohner]
innocent unschuldig [**oon**shooldig]
insect repellent Insektenschutzmittel [in**zekt**enshootsmittel] 71
insurance Versicherung [fair**zikh**eroong]
intelligent intelligent [intelli**gent**]
interpreter Dolmetscher [**dol**metsher] 79
invalid ungültig [**oon**gewltig]
Ireland Irland [**eer**lant]
Irish irisch [**ee**rish]
island Insel [**in**zel] 29, 50

J

jacket Jacke [**yak**kuh] 64
jellyfish Qualle [**kwal**luh] 53, 72
jewellery Schmuck [shmook] 66, 69
joke Scherz [shairtz]
journey Reise [**riy**zuh]
judgment Urteil [**oor**tiyl]

K

key Schlüssel [**shlew**sel] 34, 35, 39
kilo Kilo [**kee**lo] 18, 61
kilometre Kilometer [keelo**may**ter] 22
Kino Kino [**kee**no] 57
kiss Kuss [koos]
knife Messer [**mes**ser] 42
knitwear Strickwaren [**shtrik**vahren] 64

L

ladies (toilet) Damen(toilette) [**dah**men(toi**let**tuh)] 83
lake See [zay] 51
landlord Wirt [veert] 40
landscape Landschaft [**lant**shaft] 51, 56
language Sprache [**shprah**khuh] 13
large groß [grohs]
laundry Wäscherei [vesher**iy**] 65
lawn Rasen [**rah**zen]
lawyer Anwalt [**an**valt] 79
lazy faul [fowl]
leather (goods) Leder(waren) [layder(**vah**ren)] 65, 69
left links [links] 22
left-luggage office Gepäckaufbewahrung [ge**pek**owfbevahroong] 27
leg Bein [biyn] 73

length Länge [**leng**uh] 16
letter(box) Brief(kasten) [**breef**(kasten)] 81
life jacket Schwimmweste [**shvim**vestuh] 29, 55
lifebelt Rettungsring [**ret**toongsring] 29, 53
lifeboat Rettungsboot [**ret**toongsboht] 29
lift Aufzug [**owf**tsoog] 38
light *(weight)* leicht [liykht]
light *(colour)* hell [hell] 20
light *(bulb)* Licht [likht] 25, 38
linen Leinen [**liy**nen] 65
lipstick Lippenstift [**lip**penshtift] 71
litre Liter [**lee**ter] 61
little wenig [**vay**nig]
live leben [**lay**ben]; wohnen [**voh**nen]
local train Nahverkehrszug [**nah**fairkairstsoog] 27
lock Schloss [shloss]
locker Schließfach [**shlees**fakh] 27
long lang [lang]
long-distance call Ferngespräch [**fairn**geshprekh] 82
lorry Lastwagen [**last**vahgen]
lost-property office Fundbüro [**foont**bewro] 78
loud laut [lowt]
love lieben [**lee**ben]
low niedrig [**nee**drig]
luggage Gepäck [ge**pek**] 27, 32
lunch Mittagessen [**mit**tahgessen] 34, 44

M

magazine Zeitschrift [**tsiyt**shrift] 66
man Mann [man]
manager Geschäftsführer [ge**shefts**fewrer] 42
many viele [**fee**luh]
map Landkarte [**lant**kartuh] 49, 56
market(place) Markt(platz) [**markt**(plats)] 51, 60
married couple Ehepaar [**eh**uhpahr] 13
married verheiratet [fair**hiy**rahtet] 14
matches Streichhölzer [**shtriykh**herltser] 70
material Stoff [shtoff] 65
matter Sache [**za**khuh]
meal Mahlzeit [**mahl**tsiyt] 40
medicine Medikament [medika**ment**]73
memory Erinnerung [air**in**nairoong]
menu Speisekarte [**spiy**suhkartuh] 44
minute Minute [mi**noo**tuh] 18, 20
misfortune Unglück [**oon**glewk] 24
Miss Fräulein [**froy**liyn] 12
mistake Fehler [**fay**ler] 25
Mister Herr [hair] 12
mix up verwechseln [fair**vekh**zeln]
modern modern [mo**dairn**]
moment Moment [mo**ment**]
monastery Kloster [**kloh**ster]
Monday Montag [**mon**tahg] 19
money Geld [gelt] 77
month Monat [**moh**nat] 18, 19
morning Morgen [**mor**gen]; Vormittag [**for**mittahg] 20
mother Mutter [**moo**ter] 13
motor Motor [mo**tor**]
motorbike Motorrad [mo**tor**-rahd] 22, 25
motorhome Wohnmobil [**vohn**mobeel]
motorway Autobahn [**ow**tobahn] 24
mountain Berg [bairg] 50, 55
mouthwash Mundwasser [**moont**vasser] 71
museum Museum [moo**zay**-oom] 50
music Musik [moo**zik**] 57, 58

N

nail file Nagelfeile [**na**gelfiyluh] 71
nail scissors Nagelschere [**na**gelshairuh] 71
nail varnish (remover) Nagellack(entferner) [**nah**gel-lak(ent**fair**ner)] 71
nailbrush Nagelbürste [**nah**gelbewrstuh] 71
name Name [**nah**muh] 12
napkin Serviette [sair**vye**tuh] 42
nappies Windeln [**vin**deln] 71
nationality Staatsangehörigkeit [**shtahts**angeherigkiyt] 13
natural fibre Naturfaser [na**toor**fahzer] 65
nature Natur [na**toor**] 55
nausea Übelkeit [**ew**belkiyt] 72
near nahe [**nah**-uh]
necessary nötig [**ner**tig]
necklace Kette [**ket**tuh] 66
neighbour Nachbar [**nakh**bar] 13
nephew Neffe [**nef**fuh] 13
never nie [nee]
new neu [noy]

news Nachrichten [**nahkh**rikhten] 18, 82
New Zealand Neuseeland [noy**zay**lant] 13
next nächste [**naykhs**tuh]
nice *(friendly)* nett [net]; *(pretty)* schön [shern]
niece Nichte [**nikh**tuh] 13
night Nacht [nakht] 20
nightdress Nachthemd [**nakht**hemt] 64
no nein [niyn]
nobody niemand [**nee**mant]
noise Lärm [lairm]
non-smoker Nichtraucher [**nikht**rowkher] 27, 29
noon Mittag [**mit**tahg] 20
normal normal [nor**mahl**]
North Norden [**nor**den] 22
nothing nichts [nikhts]
nude nackt [nakt]
number Nummer [**noo**mer]; Zahl [tsahl]

O

of age volljährig [**foll**yairig]
office Amt [amt] 81
often oft [oft]
old alt [alt]
open geöffnet [ge-**erf**net] 81; offen [**of**fen]
opening hours Öffnungszeiten [**erf**noongstsiyten] 67, 81
opinion Meinung [**miy**noong]
optician Optiker [**op**tiker] 69
other andere [**an**deruh]
owner Besitzer [be**zit**-tser]

P

package Päckchen [**pek**-khen] 81
page Seite [**ziy**tuh]
pains Schmerzen [**shmair**tsen] 72
painting Gemälde [ge**mel**duh] 50
pair Paar [pahr] 60
palace Palast [pa**last**] 50
paper Zeitung [**tsiy**toong] 66
paper(s) Papier(e) [pa**peer**(uh)] 21, 78
parcel Paket [pak**kayt**] 81
parents Eltern [**el**tairn] 13
parking space Parkplatz [**park**plats] 23, 33, 39
part Teil [tiyl]
party Fest [fest]
passage(way) Durchgang [**doorkh**gang]
passenger Passagier [passa**sheer**] 28, 29
passport Reisepass [**riy**zuhpass] 21, 78
past Vergangenheit [fair**gang**enhiyt]
path Pfad [pfaht] 22, 55
pay zahlen [**tsah**len] 43
pedestrian Fußgänger [**foos**genger] 50
people Volk [follk]
percent Prozent [pro**tsent**] 60
perfume Parfüm [par**fewm**] 71
petrol Benzin [ben**tseen**] 24
petrol station Tankstelle [**tank**shteluh] 24
pharmacy Apotheke [apo**tay**kuh] 76
photo (shop) Foto(geschäft) [**fo**to(gesheft)] 66
picture Bild [bilt]
piece Stück [shtewk] 61
pillow Kopfkissen [**kopf**kissen] 34, 38
place Ort [ort]
places of interest Sehenswürdigkeiten [**zay**ensvewrdikiyten] 50, 52
plain Ebene [**ay**benuh] 55
plant Pflanze [**pflan**tsuh] 55, 60
plate Teller [**tel**ler] 42
platform Bahnsteig [**bahn**shtiyg] 27, 29
play spielen [**shpee**len]
please bitte [**bit**tuh]
poisonous giftig [**gif**tig]
police Polizei [poli**tsiy**] 78
policeman Polizist [poli**tsist**] 78
politics Politik [poli**tik**]
poor arm [ahrm]
port Hafen [**hah**fen]
possible möglich [**mer**glikh]
post (office) Post(amt) [**post** (amt)] 77, 81
postcard Postkarte [**post**kartuh] 81
pottery Keramik [ke**rah**mik] 51, 69
powder Puder [**poo**der] 71
pregnant schwanger [**shva**nger] 73
prescription Rezept [re**tsept**] 72
present Geschenk [ge**shenk**] 69
pretty hübsch [hewbsh]
price Preis [priys] 32, 60
profession Beruf [be**roof**] 14
programme *(television)* Sendung [**zen**doong] 82
prohibited verboten [fair**boh**ten]
pub Bierlokal [**beer**lokal]; Kneipe [**kniy**puh] 43, 48
public öffentlich [**er**fentlikh]

pull ziehen [**tsee**-en]
pullover Pullover [pull**ohver**]
punctual pünktlich [**pewnk**tlikh]
punishment Strafe [**shtrah**fuh]
purse Geldbeutel [**gelt**boytel] 78
pyjamas Schlafanzug [**shlahf**antsoog] 64

Q

quarter Stadtteil [**shtat**-tiyl] 50
question Frage [**frah**guh] 16, 17
quick schnell [shnell]
quiet(ly) leise [**liy**zuh]

R

radiator Heizkörper [**hiyts**kerper] 34
radio Radio [**rahd**yo] 39, 82
rain(coat) Regen(mantel) [**re**gen(mantel)]18, 64
rape Vergewaltigung [fairge**val**tigoong] 78
razor Rasierapparat [ra**zeer**aparaht] 66, 71
razor blades Rasierklingen [ra**zeer**klingen] 71
ready fertig [**fair**tig]
real estate Immobilien [imo**beel**yen]
reason Grund [groont]
receipt Quittung [**kwit**toong] 43, 60
recipe Rezept [re**tsept**]
recommend empfehlen [em**pfay**len]
records Schallplatten [**shal**platten] 60
relative Verwandte *(f.)* [fair**van**tuh]; Verwandter *(m.)* [fair**van**ter] 13
rent mieten [**mee**ten] 22
repeat wiederholen [veeder**hoh**len]
residence Wohnsitz [**vohn**zits]
restaurant Restaurant [resto**rant**] 40, 44
restless unruhig [**oon**roohig]
result Ergebnis [air**gayb**nis] 54, 56
rich reich [riykh]
right rechts [rekhts] 22
right (correct) richtig [**rikh**tig]
risk Risiko [**ri**ziko]
river Fluss [floos] 55
road Landstraße [**lant**shtrasuh] 22, 24
room Zimmer [**tsi**mmer] 32, 33
rotten faul [fowl]
rough seas Seegang [**zay**gang] 29
round rund [roont]
row Reihe [**riy**uh] 58
rubbish Müll [mewl] 39

S

sad traurig [**trow**rig]
safe sicher [**zi**kher]
safety belt Sicherheitsgurt [**zi**kherhiytsgoort] 22
sales Ausverkauf [**ows**fairkowf] 60
sandals Sandalen [zan**dah**len] 64
sanitary towels Damenbinden [**dah**menbinden] 71
satisfied zufrieden [tsoo**free**den]
Saturday Samstag [**zams**tahg] 19
scarf Halstuch [**hals**tookh]; Schal [shahl] 64
scissors Schere [**shair**uh] 71
Scotland Schottland [**shot**tlant] 13
Scottish schottisch [**shot**tish] 13, 40
sea Meer [mair] 53
seafood Meeresfrüchte [**maire**sfrewkhtuh] 45
seasick seekrank [**zay**krank] 29, 72
season (high/off-) Saison (Hoch-/Neben-) [zayzo (**hokh**-/**ne**ben-)]
season Jahreszeit [**yah**restsiyt] 19
seat (Sitz)Platz [(**zits**)plats] 21, 22. 40, 50, 57, 58
second Sekunde [se**koon**duh] 18, 20
self-service Selbstbedienung [**zelbst**bedeenoong] 40, 60
sell verkaufen [fair**kow**fen]
send schicken [**shik**ken]
separate(ly) getrennt [ge**trent**]
serious ernst [airnst]
service Bedienung [be**dee**noong] 41
service station Rasthaus [**rast**hows] 32
ship Schiff [shiff] 29, 30
shirt Hemd [hemt] 64
shoe (shop) Schuh(geschäft) [**shoo**(gesheft)] 61, 64
shoelaces Schuhbänder [**shoo**bender] 64
shop Geschäft [ge**sheft**]; Laden [**lah**den] 60
shop window Schaufenster [sh**ow**fenster] 60
shopping centre Einkaufszentrum [**iyn**kowfstsentroom] 60
shopping Einkaufen [**iyn**kowfen] 60
short kurz [koorts]
shower Dusche [**doo**shuh] 38
shy schüchtern [**shewkh**tern]
sightseeing tour Besichtigung [be**zeekh**tigoong]; Rundfahrt [**roont**fahrt] 49, 50, 52

sign Schild [shilt] 23, 29, 54
signature Unterschrift [**oon**tershrift] 21, 77
silence Ruhe [**roo**-uh]
silk Seide [**ziy**duh] 65
single ledig [**lay**dig]
sister Schwester [**shves**ter] 13
sister-in-law Schwägerin [**shvay**gerin] 13
situation Situation [zitoo-ats**yon**]
skirt Rock [rock] 64
sky Himmel [**him**mel] 18
sleep schlafen [**shlah**fen]
sleeping car Schlafwagen [**shlahf**vahgen] 27, 29
sleeve Ärmel [**air**mel] 64
slim schlank [shlank]
slow(ly) langsam [**lang**zam]
small klein [kliyn]
smell Geruch [ge**rookh**] 40, 44
smoke rauchen *(v.)* [**row**khen] 70
soap Seife [**ziy**fuh] 39, 71
socks Socken [**zok**ken] 64
soft weich [viykh]
soil Erde [**air**duh]
solid fest [fest]
some einige [**iy**niguh]
somebody jemand [**yay**mant]
son Sohn [zohn] 13
sorry Entschuldigung! [ent**shool**digoong] 13, 14
South Süden [**zew**den] 22
souvenirs Souvenirs [**zoo**veneers] 69
speak sprechen [**shpre**khen]
special offer Sonderangebot [**zon**derange**boht**] 60
special rate Sondertarif [**zon**derta**reef**] 29
specialities Spezialitäten [shpetsyali**tay**ten] 44, 48
speed Geschwindigkeit [gesh**vin**dikiyt] 17, 24
sponge Schwamm [shvam] 71
spoon Löffel [**ler**fel] 42
sports (articles) Sport(artikel) [**shport**(artikel)] 54
sports ground Sportplatz [**shport**plats] 54
spot Stelle [**shtel**luh]
spring *(time of year)* Frühling [**frew**ling] 19
spring *(water)* Quelle [**kwel**luh] 55
stairs Treppe [**trep**puh] 38
stamp Briefmarke [**breef**markuh] 81
start Start [shtart]
starter Vorspeise [**for**shpiysuh] 45
station Bahnhof [**bahn**hof] 27, 29
stay Aufenthalt [**ow**fenthalt] 15
steep steil [shtiyl]
stockings Strümpfe [**shtrewm**pfuh] 64
stone Stein [shtiyn]
stop Haltestelle [**hal**tuhshtelluh] 27, 30
storm Sturm [shtoorm] 18, 55
story Erzählung [air**tsay**loong]
straight on geradeaus [geraduh-**ows**]
street Straße [**shtrah**suh]
street map Stadtplan [**shtat**plahn] 49, 56
student Student [shtoo**dent**] 13
stupid dumm [doomm]
suburb Vorort [**for**ort]
subway Unterführung [oonter**fewr**oong] 23
suede Wildleder [**vilt**leder] 65, 69
suit *(for women)* Kostüm [kos**tewm**]; *(for men)* Anzug [**an**tsoog] 64
suitcase Koffer [**kof**fer] 27, 32
sum Summe [**zoo**muh]
summer Sommer [**zom**mer] 19
sun Sonne [**zon**uh]
sunburn Sonnenbrand [**zon**nenbrant]
Sunday Sonntag [**zon**tahg] 19
sunglasses Sonnenbrille [**zon**nenbrilluh] 69
suntan lotion Sonnenmilch [**zon**nenmilkh] 53, 55
supermarket Supermarkt [**zoo**permarkt] 60
supper Abendessen [**ah**bentessen] 34, 44
surprise Überraschung [ewber-**rash**oong]
sweat schwitzen [**shwi**tsen]
sweater Pullover [pull**over**] 64
sweets Süßwaren [**zews**vahren] 47
swimming pool Schwimmbad [**shvim**baht] 53
swimming trunks Badehose [**bah**duh-hohzuh] 53, 64
swimsuit Badeanzug [**bah**duhantsoog] 53, 64
Swiss Schweizer(in) [**shviy**tser(in)]
Switzerland Schweiz [shwiyts]

T

table Tisch [tish] 40
tablets Tabletten [tab**let**ten] 75, 76
take nehmen [**nay**men]
taken *(seat)* besetzt [be**setst**]
take pictures fotografieren [fotogra**fee**ren]
tall groß [grohs]
tampons Tampons [**tam**pons] 71
taste Geschmack [ge**shmak**] 40, 44
taxi Taxi [**ta**xi] 31
telegram Telegramm [tele**gram**] 82
telephone (book) Telefon(buch) [tele**fon**(bookh)] 82, 83
temperature Temperatur [tempaira**toor**] 16, 72
terrible schrecklich [**shrek**likh]
thank you danke [**dan**kuh]
theatre Theater [tay**ah**ter] 51, 57, 58
theft Diebstahl [**deep**stahl] 79
thick dick [dick]
thin dünn [dewn]
thing Ding [ding]; Sache [**zak**khuh]
thirst Durst [doorst] 48
this diese *(f.)* [**dee**zuh], dieser *(m.)* [**dee**zer], dieses *(n.)* [**dee**zes]
thunderstorm Gewitter [**ge**vitter] 18
Thursday Donnerstag [**don**nerstahg] 19
ticket *(entrance)* Eintrittskarte [**iyn**tritskartuh] 52, 57
ticket *(train, bus)* Fahrkarte [**fahr**kartuh] 27, 30
ticket machine Kartenautomat [**kar**tenowtomaht] 27, 30
tie Krawatte [kra**vat**tuh] 64
tights Strumpfhose [**shtroompf**hohzuh] 64
time *(clock)* Uhrzeit [**oor**tsiyt] 18
time Zeit [tsiyt] 18
timetable Fahrplan [**fahr**plahn] 27, 30
tip Trinkgeld [**trink**gelt] 43, 83
tired müde [**mew**duh]
tobacco Tabak [ta**bak**] 70
tobacconist Tabakladen [ta**bak**lahden] 70
together zusammen [tsoo**zam**men]
toilet Toilette [toi**let**tuh] 71, 83
too much zu viel [tsoo**feel**]
toothbrush Zahnbürste [**tsahn**bewrstuh] 71
toothpaste Zahnpasta [**tsahn**pasta] 71
tourist Tourist(in) [too**rist**(in)] 13
tourist information office Fremdenverkehrsamt [fremdenfair**kairs**amt] 49
towel Handtuch [**hant**-tookh] 38
tower Turm [toorm] 51
town centre Stadtzentrum [**shtat**-tsentroom] 50
town hall Rathaus [**raht**hows] 51
town Stadt [shtat]
toy(shop) Spielzeug(laden) [**shpeel**tsoyg(lahden)] 60
tracksuit Jogginganzug [**jog**gingantsoog] 64
traffic Verkehr [fair**kair**] 23
traffic jam Stau [shtow] 23
traffic lights Ampel [**am**pel] 22
train Zug [tsoog] 27
trainers Turnschuhe [**toorn**shoo-uh] 61, 64
tram Straßenbahn [**shtrah**senbahn] 30
travel agency Reisebüro [**riy**zuhbewro] 49, 52
travel guide Reiseführer [**riy**zuhfewrer] 49
traveller's cheque Reisescheck [**riy**zuhshek] 77
tree Baum [bowm] 55
trip Ausflug [**ows**floog] 52
trolley Kofferkuli [koffer**koo**lee] 27
trousers Hose [**hoh**zuh] 64
true wahr [vahr]
try versuchen [fair**zoo**khen]
Tuesday Dienstag [**deens**tahg] 19
tunnel Tunnel [too**nell**] 27
tweezers Pinzette [pin**tset**tuh] 71
typical typisch [**tew**pish]
tyre Reifen [**riy**fen] 26

U

ugly hässlich [**hess**likh]
umbrella Schirm [sheerm] 60
uncle Onkel [onkel] 13
underground U-Bahn [**oo**bahn] 30
underpants Unterhose [**oon**terhohzuh] 64
understand verstehen [fair**shtay**en]
underwear Unterwäsche [**oon**terveshuh] 64
unhappy unglücklich [**oon**glewklikh]
unknown unbekannt [**oon**bekant]
urgent dringend [**dring**ent]

V

valid gültig [**gew**ltig]
value Wert [vairt]
vantage point Aussichtspunkt [**ows**zikhtspoonkt] 50, 55
vegetable Gemüse [ge**mew**zuh] 47, 62
very sehr [zayr]
vest Unterhemd [**oon**terhemt] 64
view Aussicht [**ows**zikht] 50, 55
village Dorf [dorf] 22
visibility Sicht [zikht]

W

wait (for) warten (auf) [**var**ten (owf)]
waiter Kellner [**kel**ner]; Ober [**oh**ber] 41
waiting room Wartezimmer [**var**tuhtsimmer] 72
waitress Kellnerin [**kel**nerin] 41
Wales Wales [**va**les] 13
walk Spaziergang *(n.)* [shpa**tseer**gang] 55
walk zu Fuß gehen *(v.)* [tsoo foos **gay**en]
wallet Brieftasche [**breef**tashuh] 79
want wollen [**vol**len]
warm warm [varm]
warranty Garantie [garan**tee**] 60
wash waschen [**va**shen] 65, 70
washing-up liquid Spülmittel [**shpewl**mittel] 71
watch (shop) Uhr(macherladen) [**oor**(makherlahden)] 66, 79
water Wasser [**vas**ser] 37, 39, 48
wave Welle [**vel**luh] 53, 55
way Weg [vayg]
weather Wetter [**vet**ter] 18
weather report Wettervorhersage [vetterfor**hair**zahguh] 18, 82
wedding Hochzeit [**hokh**tsiyt]
Wednesday Mittwoch [**mit**vokh] 19
week Woche [**vo**khuh]19, 20
weekdays werktags [**vairk**tahgs] 19
weigh wiegen [**vee**gen]
weight Gewicht [ge**veekht**] 16
wellingtons Gummistiefel [**goo**mi**shtee**fel] 61, 64
Welsh walisisch [va**lee**sish] 13, 40
West Westen [**ves**ten] 22
wet nass [nas]
when wenn [ven]
wide breit [briyt]
wife Ehefrau [**eh**uh frow] 12, 13
winter Winter [**vin**ter] 19
wish wünschen [**vewn**shen]
witness Zeuge [**tsoy**guh] 24, 78
woman Frau [frow]
wood Holz [holts] 37
wool Wolle [**vol**luh] 65
word Wort [vort]
work Arbeit [**ar**biyt] 15
world Welt [velt]
wrong falsch [falsh]

Y

year Jahr [yahr] 18
yes ja [yah]
young jung [yoong]
youth hostel Jugendherberge [**yoo**genthairbairguh] 38

Z

zip Reißverschluss [**riys**vairshloos] 60

German–English A–Z

A

Abfahrt departure
Abflug departure *(airport)*
abgesagt cancelled
Achtung caution
Ankunft arrival
Anmeldeschein *(hotel)* registration form
Apotheke chemist
Ausfahrt (freihalten) clear keep
Ausgang exit; way out
Auskunft information
Auslandsflüge international flights
Ausstellung exhibition
ausverkauft sold out
Autobahn motorway
Autovermietung car rental

B
Bäckerei bakery
Bahnhof station
Bahnsteig platform
Bank bank
Bedarfshaltestelle request stop
Benzin petrol
besetzt engaged
Bitte einordnen get in lane
Briefe letters
Briefmarken stamps
Buchladen bookseller
Bushaltestelle bus stop
Busspur bus lane

C
Campingplatz camping site

D
Damen (toilette) ladies' (toilet)
defekt out of order
Drogerie chemist
Drücken press (button), push (door)
Durchgang verboten no access

E
Einbahnstraße one-way street
Eingang entrance
Eingang für Rollstuhlfahrer wheelchair access
einspuriger Verkehr single-file traffic
Einsteigen boarding
Eintritt (frei) admission (free)
Einzelfahrkarte single
Erdgeschoß ground floor
Erfrischungen refreshments
Ermäßigung concession
Erste Hilfe first aid
Erwachsene (nur für) adults (only)

F
Fahrplan timetable
Fahrradvermietung bicycle hire
Fahrstuhl lift
Familienstand marital status
Feiertag bank holiday
Feuerlöscher fire extinguisher
Feuerwehr fire brigade
Fischgeschäft fishmonger
Flughafen airport
frei vacant
Frisch gestrichen wet paint
Friseur hairdresser
Fundbüro lost-property office
Fußgängerüberweg pedestrian crossing
Fußgängerzone pedestrian precinct

G
Gefahr danger
Geldwechsel bureau de change
geöffnet open
geschlossen closed
Geschwindigkeitsbegrenzung speed limit
gestrichen cancelled
gratis free
gültig (ab) (valid from)

H
Hafen harbour, port
Handarbeit hand-made
Herein Come in
Herren (toilette) gentlemen's
Herrenfriseur barber
hier zahlen (Kasse) pay here (till)

I
Information information
Inlandflüge domestic flights

K
Kein Trinkwasser not drinking water
kein Zutritt private
Keine Rückgabe von Wechselgeld change not given
Keine Zimmer frei no vacancies
Keller basement
Kreisverkehr roundabout
Kreuzung crossroads

L
Langsam fahren drive slowly
langsam slow
Langsamer fahren reduce speed now
Leerung (post) collection
Links abbiegen verboten no left turn

M
Mehrwertsteuer value added tax
Metzgerei butcher
mit Verspätung delayed

N
Name name
Nicht berühren Do not touch

Nichtraucher no smoking
Normal(benzin) bleifrei unleaded petrol
Notausgang emergency exit
Notbremse emergency brake

O

Öffnungszeiten opening hours
Optiker optician

P

Parkhaus car park
Parkplatz car park
Parkuhr meter
Parkverbot no parking
Pension bed and breakfast
Polizei police
Postamt post office
postlagernde Sendungen poste restante
Praxis surgery
privat private
Privatzimmer bed and breakfast

R

Rastplatz lay-by
Rathaus town hall
Raucher smoker
Reisebüro travel agent
Reisepaß passport
Rezeption reception
Rückfahrkarte return ticket

S

Sackgasse dead end
Schlafwagen sleeping car
Schlußverkauf sale
Schnellstraße dual carriageway
Schwimmbad swimming pool
Selbstbedienung self-service
Sonderangebot special offer
Sparkasse savings bank
Speisekarte menu
Speisewagen restaurant car
Sprechzimmer surgery
Staatsangehörigkeit nationality
Stau traffic jam
Stockwerk floor
Straßenarbeiten roadworks
Super bleifrei super unleaded petrol
Super verbleit four-star petrol

T

Tabakwarenladen tobacconist
Tagesgericht dish of the day
Tagesmenü set menu
Toiletten toilets
Touristeninformation tourist information office
Transitschalter transit desk
Treffpunkt meeting point

U

U-Bahn Underground
Umkleidekabinen fitting rooms
Umleitung diversion
Unterschrift signature

V

verboten prohibited
verkaufen (zu) for sale
verspätet delayed
Vorfahrt beachten give way
Vorverkauf advance bookings

W

Warteraum lounge; waiting room
Wartesaal waiting room
Wäscherei laundry

Z

Zentrum centre
Ziehen pull (door)
Zimmer frei rooms vacant
Zoll customs
zollpflichtige Waren goods to declare
Zutritt verboten no entry
Zweitaktmischung two-stroke

Photo credits

ACE/Mauritius: cover; Apa/Robin Lawrence: 1, 57, 60; Apa/Mark Read: 49, 68; Apa/Dirk Renckhoff: 17R, 21; Apa/Phil Wood: 17L, 36, 40; Herbert Hartmann: 12, 25, 32, 66, 72, 77; Bob Krist: 80; Erhard Pansegrau: 53.